PERSONAL
EFFECTIVENESS

The Effective Supervisory Management Series

The Effective Supervisory Management Series provides a step-by-step guide to every aspect of the modern supervisory manager's role. Comprising three books, all of which have been completely revised and up-dated in their second editions, the series gives comprehensive coverage of the following syllabuses:

- **National Examining Board for Supervisory Management (NEBSM) — formerly NEBSS — Supervisory Management Certificate**
- **The Institute of Supervisory Management (ISM) Certificate in Supervisory Management Studies**
- **The Institute of Bankers (IOB) Banking Certificate – "Supervisory Skills" and Diploma — "Nature of Management".**

Specially designed for use by supervisors at all levels of responsibility, these three books can be used individually or as a reference pack to be consulted time and time again. Each chapter commences with a set of objectives which, by the end of the chapter, the reader will have achieved. Focusing on state-of-the-art management methods, particularly those involving information technology and the crucially important Codes of Practice which affect managerial issues, each chapter then concludes with a succinct summary of the key points.

The three books in the series are:

Managing People
Managing Activities and Resources
Personal Effectiveness

PERSONAL
EFFECTIVENESS

**SECOND
EDITION**

ROGER BENNETT

KOGAN
PAGE

First published in 1989 by
Kogan Page Ltd, in association with
the National Extension College,
18 Brooklands Avenue, Cambridge CB2 2HN, and
the Institute of Supervisory Management,
22 Bore Street, Lichfield, Staffordshire WS13 6LP.
This edition published in 1994 by Kogan Page Ltd.

Kogan Page Limited
120 Pentonville Road
London N1 9JN

British Library Cataloguing in Publication Data
A CIP record for this book is available
from the British Library.

ISBN 0 7494 1266 6

Typeset by Photoprint, Torquay, South Devon
Printed in England by Clays Ltd, St Ives plc

Contents

Extracts from the Preface to the First Edition

The three books in this series are about practical management skills, particularly those interpersonal supervisory skills which enable managers to communicate effectively, influence others, lead, plan, coordinate and control. More than ever before, business requires managers who are formally trained and competent in practical administrative technique: in skills that are anchored against *occupationally relevant* competencies immediately applicable in any sort of organisation, and not against abstract theories and applications suited mainly to the needs of very large firms. The books attempt to combine theory with practice and to provide the reader with a working knowledge of current legislation relevant to the supervisory management field, of management concepts and the latest techniques.

Together the three books comprise a skills building programme designed to springboard a newly appointed or junior manager — concerned primarily with supervisory and executive management — to a level of competence at which he or she can assume a more responsible role. After reading these books you should be able to undertake a variety of useful practical management tasks: counsel, make a presentation, chair a meeting, write a job description, negotiate, appraise the performances of employees, and so on.

I gratefully acknowledge the permission granted by the editors of *Modern Management*, the *Training Officer* and *Export* for the use of materials previously published in these journals in article form. Parts of Chapter 3 and 7 are based on material prepared for my Pitman text *Organisation and Management*. I thank Pitman Publishing for their kind permission to adapt this material. Thanks are also due to the Equal Opportunities Commission for permission to reproduce parts of its Code of Practice on the avoidance of discrimination in employment.

Preface to the Second Edition

These new editions of the three books in the *Effective Supervisory Management* series contain fresh material on a number of recently introduced EC Directives; empowerment; the use of visual aids when making presentations; government guidelines concerning the treatment of employees with HIV; flexible working methods and just-in-time procedures; total quality management; and the 1993 Health and Safety at Work Regulations. Legal references plus the sections on maternity pay and SSP have been revised and updated.

I am indebted to Rosalind Bailey for word-processing the amendments to the manuscript, and to Kogan Page Ltd for their efficient processing of the texts.

Roger Bennett

1
Making a Presentation

Objectives

This chapter will help you to:

- overcome the problems associated with public speaking
- make effective use of visual aids
- prepare for a presentation, including writing speeches and anticipating questions.

Most managers are required at least occasionally to address groups of people. Common examples are team briefings, giving instructions to several workers at a time, training activities, making a formal presentation of a new proposal to senior management, making short speeches when colleagues retire, and in committees and other meetings. Many managers dread these situations. They have no experience of public speaking, and are fearful of the responses their efforts might invoke. This is unfortunate because the ability to speak confidently before a group is an extremely valuable interpersonal management skill. In this chapter I shall seek to convince you that the techniques of effective verbal communication can be learned and give you enough background to enable you independently to attempt a presentation.

Of all the ways you communicate with others the manner of your speech conveys most directly how you think and feel. Body language, posture, dress and gesture contribute to the impressions you create, but your speaking voice is, above all,

Activity

What experience have you had of public speaking and what aspects worry you the most?

Your personal experience may vary considerably. Some of you may lead very active social lives and serve on several committees. Some of you may be members of debating societies and regularly speak in public. Some of you may dread being called upon to contribute to a debate and never volunteer an answer.

The main fear is that of being made to look stupid in front of others, of drying up or being unable to move. In this chapter you will be shown some of the techniques and skills of public speaking. There is no shame attached to feeling nervous, but this should not prevent you from playing an active role at a meeting, or presenting a proposal etc.

the means whereby you project your true identity. You must learn, therefore, to use your voice — to intonate, respond to the cues of others, pause at appropriate moments and so on. When addressing a group, speak *slowly*. A pace that you regard as slow will in fact be perceived as normal by an audience which has both to *assimilate* what you say and *interpret* your emotions. Thus, intentionally pace your speed of delivery and consciously articulate each word. It seems strange at first, but it will result in clear and unhesitant delivery, since you will emphasise the words most relevant to your meaning.

Nerves

Fear is a natural physiological response to threatening situations. It tells you to get away from a potentially harmful environment. Apprehension about speaking before others is caused by a mixture of misgivings about the suitability of your style of presentation for the particular audience, your ability to make the presentation, your appearance or about the possible consequences of a hostile reception. Unfortunately, the voice is extremely sensitive to feelings of unease and will emit distress signals such as quivering, a high pitched tone, loss of inflexion etc in moments of stress. The neck, throat and tongue become tense; you dry up, physically as well as emotionally. To overcome anxiety you must relax and rationalise the situation. When fear overcomes you, pause; breathe slowly; deliberately loosen your head, neck and shoulder muscles, starting from the top of your head and working down. The audience will not notice the interruption: to them it is simply a natural pause in the flow of the presentation. Look directly at the friendliest face in the audience. If you begin to tremble, increase your use of body language in order to dissipate the surplus energy. Then smile. This will help you to relax and generally connect with the audience.

Remember always that the audience *wants* to hear what you have to say, and bear in mind that you have the *right* to express an opinion. You are fully entitled to be taken seriously! If you honestly *believe* in what you are saying and in your fundamental right to state a firm position then mistakes and minor inadequacies in your presentation will not become too important in your own mind. It is vital, however, that you prepare your talk diligently and in great detail. While it is not appropriate to read a speech verbatim, the existence of a script in front of you offers an escape route in moments of crisis. The instant you begin to lose control, refer to your notes and before you know it your fear will have begun to subside.

Self-check

What happens when you are nervous and how can you overcome fear?

Answer

The symptoms will depend on the individual, but broadly speaking nerves will cause you to tense up, your mouth to become dry and your voice to quiver.

The only solution is to try to relax. If water is available, take a sip. Take deep breaths.

Preparation

Do not attempt to make a presentation if you do not know what you are talking about. The audience will soon recognise your ignorance and your integrity will be questioned. At the end of the presentation you normally have to take questions and if you cannot handle these your credibility is destroyed. Analyse your potential audience. Are they likely to be well informed on the subject? How easily will they absorb the material you need to present? Are they capable of concentrating for long periods? Who will be present and what will be their likely state of mind? Plan the talk. Draft an outline with sections for the introduction, a statement of your proposition, supporting arguments and recommendations. Then fill out each section as fully as you can. Predetermine a central thesis that will run through the entire presentation and to which all comments will relate. Normally, you speak at the rate of about 150 words per minute, so your introductory remarks should be no more than one or two minutes long. The introduction could be an anecdote, a rhetorical question or a controversial remark. Begin your notes with a precise definition of the topic you wish to discuss and then write a formal declaration (without justification at this point) of your feelings or position on the subject. You should then explain why you are giving the talk, leading on to detailed consideration of issues. Make your points one by one, with examples, evidence and justifications of previous assertions. All your points should relate to the central thesis, and lead you towards a clearly defined conclusion which should be firmly stated and take no more than a couple of minutes (about 300 words) to present. Then summarise the *major* features of your argument. It is always wise to prepare more material than you think you will need and be sure to segment it into a visibly logical progression.

Presentation

Dwell on the *fundamental* points that you wish to drive home. You may repeat these (perhaps using different words) several times during the talk. Speak to the whole of the audience and consciously modulate your voice. It does not matter which particular regional accent influences your manner of speech, but a well-modulated talk carries conviction and credibility and creates favourable images of the speaker. Your *sincerity* and *enthusiasm* are transmitted to the audience in this way. Try to project your voice to the back of the room without shouting. Do not mumble or allow your voice to fade. Whenever you begin to sound hoarse, pause for a drink of water.

If you use a white or black board or flip chart, be sure you continue to address the audience and not the visual aid. Otherwise you become inaudible while (discourteously) presenting your back to the audience. Stand in front of rather than behind a desk, since the presence of a desk creates a psychological barrier between you and your listeners. Avoid lazy speech, especially phrases such as 'you know' and 'ers' and 'ums', during the presentation. Try to appear friendly and pleasant since these emotions induce positive responses from other people. Apathy in an audience can be quite disconcerting so if you sense this happening, introduce a joke or humorous story. However, *never* assume that a joke will be an integral part of a presentation, since each audience is unique and you may quickly realise that its mood may not be conducive to the joke you have written.

Timing is important. Stick to the schedule laid down in your written notes and remember that the span of attention of the average person is quite short (concentration wanders usually after about 15 minutes). Do not be afraid therefore to insert the occasional controversial statement to surprise the audience or otherwise stimulate its attention. Intersperse short sentences with long ones.

Body language

Most speakers feel more at ease if their body weight falls mainly on one foot rather than standing 'at attention', or 'lolling' around. Body language can be as influential as the words you use, so make sure you are smartly dressed and avoid inappropriate gestures. Do not speak with your hands in your pockets (which creates an impression of nervousness), and use hand movements sparingly. Shift your body position occasionally, but do not touch your face, scratch or wag your finger. Rather, use gestures to reinforce important points. For example, you might fully raise both eyebrows and/or open your arms to indicate disbelief or look downwards while expressing anger. Crossing the arms or legs usually creates a defensive impression, 'opening up' the arms does the opposite. If you are nervous, the best starting position is probably with your arms hanging loosely by your sides, since this will help your upper body to relax. To the extent you use gestures, make the gesture first and follow it up with a verbal comment.

Aim to project an image of relaxed competence. Do not fidget. Be aware of what you are doing with your hands, bearing in mind that excessive arm and hand waving can be extremely disconcerting to others. Body language may overwhelm verbal messages. Wearing the wrong clothes, for instance, can lead to disaster. Suppose you had to make a farewell speech at a colleague's retirement function and you turned up casually dressed, only to find everyone else formally attired!

Persuasion

On occasion, you will have to convince an audience of the correctness of a position, or that its members should willingly accept a change. In these cases, you cannot simply allow the facts to speak for themselves; you must also express opinions. Special principles apply to the practice of persuasive advocacy:

- use plenty of illustrations to support your case. Quote several different examples to reinforce the same point
- begin the body of the talk with subject matter that the audience will agree with. Once people have started to agree with you — no matter how trivial your initial comments — they are likely to continue agreeing with you when more controversial topics are introduced. Proceed from the known and agreed to the unknown and controversial
- explain rather than argue your case. Do not draw attention to the existence of alternative interpretations of the issue

- motivate the audience into acceptance of the proposition by pointing out how it will benefit audience members.

When attempting to persuade, you should if possible be aware of the audience's current or anticipated views and of how its members perceive your role. If you are known and liked by the group and if the group normally expects you to initiate activity then you will be more likely to influence its opinions. It may be best to present both sides of the argument to the audience, pointing out the problems associated with your own position. This creates impressions of knowledgeability, sincerity, integrity and even-handedness on your part. Treat the audience with respect. Drop the occasional compliment.

Persuasive talks are more difficult than others because you have to ask the audience to give you something, even if it is only their emotional support. And the audience could turn hostile! Allow for this possibility in your initial planning. Predict likely objections and have an alternative set of less controversial points available for discussion.

Visual aids

Visual aids serve two functions. They clarify issues and hence reduce the number of words that need to be spoken and they help the speaker segment a talk into natural divisions. Although visual aids can greatly impress an audience, there is a danger that the aids themselves instead of the speaker might become the focus of the audience's attention and they can actually distract an audience. Used properly, visual aids:

- add variety to the presentation
- create interest and enthusiasm among the audience
- create an impression of competence on your part
- reinforce key concepts
- stimulate audience involvement with the discussion
- increase the audience's rate of retention of information
- help you complete the talk faster and in a logical manner.

They are particularly useful where complex diagrams or technical details are essential to the presentation. Aids should be large enough to be clearly visible to all parts of the audience and each diagram, heading or statement should be self-contained, clear and relevant to the discussion. Do not introduce visual aids too early in the talk. Try first to create verbally a general context to which each aid can be related. Tell the audience what the aid is intended to demonstrate and explain its significance to the point being discussed. If you can introduce a new visual (say) once every seven or eight minutes, your talk will be well segmented, but do not use aids merely for their own sake. Each should have a definite and identifiable purpose.

The overhead projector

Overhead transparencies are by far the most common visual aid used during presentations. They focus the audience's attention and reinforce verbal messages. The following rules should be applied when using an overhead projector (OHP).

- Do not use an OHP to present a simple point that could be put across better by a verbal statement.
- Restrict the amount of information placed on any one transparency. Complex tables are best put into handouts (see below). If tables are necessary, they need to be short, and the numbers within them kept to just three or four digits.
- Look at the audience while the transparency is being shown, not at the screen. Maintain eye contact with the audience.
- Turn off the OHP as soon as you have finished discussing the information on the transparency. Only switch on again when you need to present a further transparency.
- Do not use more than five or six lines of text per transparency, and use large letters: text that is too small to read is totally useless.
- Do not merely read out the words on the transparency; discuss generally the point to which they refer.
- Position the OHP slightly to the side of the centre of the room, while yourself retaining the central position. Hence *you* remain the focal point of the presentation.

Handouts

If you need to present detailed information to an audience, this is frequently best achieved *via* a handout distributed before, during or after your talk. Use of handouts leaves you free to concentrate on major points, which are then reinforced by the materials handed out. A problem with handouts is how to ensure they are read. Handouts distributed at the close of a presentation are likely to be taken home and forgotten. Everyone *intends* reading a handout at the first convenient moment, but relatively few people actually get around to doing it! If conversely the material is given out during or at the start of the presentation the recipients are likely to read it while you are talking and not listen to what is actually being said. Also the process of distributing material during a presentation can itself be highly disruptive.

Awkward questions

Always assume that someone in the audience will ask the question you *least* want to answer. Before the presentation, write out a list of likely questions and prepare model answers. When a hostile question is asked, try if possible to agree with at least one aspect of the speaker's comments. Never be discourteous to the questioner; the audience is far more likely to side with that person than with you. If you can, emphathise with the questioner. Ask yourself why the questioner feels that way. It is better to take questions at the end of, rather than during, a presentation.

Give as much additional information as you possibly can in each of your answers. A good technique for answering questions is to restate each question asked but in your own words. You say, 'The question asks . . .', and then interpret the questioner's meaning. This acts as a check on your understanding of the question, it indicates that you are taking the questioner seriously, it gives you time to think, ensures that everyone hears the question and focuses the audience's attention on you rather than the questioner. Divide a complicated question into its constituent parts and give a separate answer to each component.

Activity

How do you deal with hostile and awkward questions? What do you do if you do not know the answer?

In preparing for the presentation, it is always a good idea to anticipate what questions are likely to be asked and how you intend to respond. While an awkward question may be one that is difficult to answer, a hostile question is put in order to provoke the presenter.

In dealing with questions, try to be polite at all times, no matter how unpleasantly the question is worded. If you cannot answer the question, it is better to admit it, rather than bluff your way out. Ask for time to consider the question but if you promise to look into the matter, remember to do so. Failure to keep such a promise will affect your credibility with the audience.

Answer the questions asked, but do not enter into a dialogue with members of the audience. If you do not know the answer to a question, say so and provide a reason for your not knowing. You might even congratulate a questioner for uncovering an aspect of the problem you had not previously considered. Promise to investigate the matter and to reply more fully in due course, perhaps in writing. Do not reply to abusive questions; simply ask for the next question. If the abuse continues you should restate your purpose in offering the presentation, your qualifications for being in front of the group and then state why you consider the question to be irrelevant or why for some other reason it should not be answered. Address your remarks to the entire audience rather than the individual questioner. If someone tries to give a speech from the floor, interrupt and ask for a statement of the question. Above all, never lose your temper.

Using presentation skills

Briefing sessions

Team briefings seek to transmit information about decisions that have *already* been taken or events that have already occurred. In a briefing, you aim not only to impart news, but also to instil in employees a sense of participation in the organisation's affairs. Sessions should be short (about ten minutes, plus perhaps five more for questions) and cover such topics as:

- changes in working arrangements
- news of staff transfers and promotions
- results of implementation of new working methods
- details of new recreational/welfare facilities
- examples of how efficiency has been improved in other departments
- news about how the organisation is progressing generally, including plans for the future.

Briefing sessions are not suitable, however, for collective bargaining or for the discussion of fundamental issues about terms and conditions of employment. Aim to brief your section at predetermined intervals, say once every two months, rather than irregularly — assuming of course that on each occasion you have some significant information to communicate. A common mistake is for managers to brief their subordinates only at times of crisis, so that briefing sessions transmit only negative information and views. Sessions should be relatively informal, but structured, preplanned and systematic. Team briefings are better than staff circulars, magazines or other written material because of the personal face to face contact they require. Circulars rarely include *everything* that needs to be said about an issue. They cannot emphasise all the significant points and they might not be read by affected parties. Note that a briefing session is an *event* to employees. The fact that you have announced and organised the session implies that you have substantial news to transmit and people will feel let down if the information turns out to be trivial.

Tell your team where and when the briefing will take place, what it will be about and why you have called the session. The best time for a briefing session is perhaps just before lunch. People are relatively fresh and no extra time is involved in restarting work at the end of the briefing. In order to create a sense of occasion, hold the session (if possible) in a room away from the work place. The room should be comfortable — and have enough chairs, otherwise you will waste time collecting chairs from other rooms and in so doing you will diminish the dignity of the meeting. Arrange the chairs in a semi-circular pattern (I assume you are dealing with about 12–15 subordinates) and sit (rather than stand) facing them at approximately the same distance from them as they are from each other. You will then be seen as an integral part of the group rather than as someone giving instructions. Copies of relevant documents should be available at the session.

Begin by saying why you called the meeting, give the facts, quote examples, and highlight the major features of the issue. Your aim is to transmit information clearly and quickly, so pre-empt as many questions as possible by providing the answers to likely questions in the main body of your presentation.

Self-check

What is the purpose of team briefing sessions?

Answer
The main purpose is to transmit information about decisions already taken. Ideally these sessions should be held regularly rather than simply when there is a crisis. However, care must be taken to ensure that the matters dealt with are not considered trivial by staff, or they will view the sessions as a waste of time.

A presentation to a retiring colleague

Sooner or later, someone in your department will reach retirement age and, naturally, you will be expected as section leader to make a short speech at the retirement presentation. Nowadays, we tend to speak in simpler and more direct terms at such functions than previously has been the case, without an elaborate introduction and without flowery language. Never alter your accent or manner of speaking or use long words you would not normally employ. You will come across as silly and 'affected' if you do. The following points should be included in the presentation.

- An expression of how much the colleague will be missed.
- The person's contributions over the years and his or her special characteristics (courtesy, kindness, willingness to help others, etc).
- A brief outline of the colleague's career.
- A mention of the person's outside interests and what he or she will be doing when retired.
- Best wishes for the future.

Contributing to a committee meeting

You attend a management committee meeting the agenda of which contains an item you particularly want to discuss. The item is introduced from the chair, other people comment, the point approaches where you feel you ought to interject. Your heart pounds, your mouth is dry, you blush, breathe quickly, your throat is tight and your hands tremble slightly. You try to speak, but your voice quivers. Your mind is blank, you cannot even remember the points you intended raising. Instead of contributing to the discussion, you make a single inane remark before hurriedly withdrawing to the anonymity of silence. You conform totally to the views of others, though after the meeting you feel deeply unhappy about the decision finally taken.

Most managers have experienced this situation as least once in their careers — for some it is a common occurrence. To overcome such emotional reactions you need to understand why you lose control. Usually, these feelings are triggered by one of two categories of anxiety: fear of humiliation or of adverse consequences that might result from your intervention. People who are friends, who converse and interact socially outside a meeting will typically behave differently towards each other once a meeting has begun. You need therefore to shift your consciousness during meetings. Accept that once you begin to address the meeting you become separated from the group. Temporarily, you and not the chairperson are its leader. As a silent member you are anonymous and unthreatened: you cannot be embarrassed or overwhelmed by the situation — but as a speaker, you are exposed and vulnerable — your (self created) image of yourself is put to the test and becomes subject to external attack. Thus, you have to switch (consciously) from one mode of behaviour — the informal conversational approach which you adopt in your normal day to day activities — to a formal communications role. You can only do this effectively if you prepare meticulously for the meeting. If you feel that preparation is not worthwhile, then you should seriously consider whether it is worth attending the meeting. There are three steps involved in preparation: analysis of the 'audience', analysis of the agenda and drafting your intended comments.

Audience analysis

First, analyse the context in which the meeting is to occur. What purpose is the meeting intended to serve? Why are the other members attending? What benefits might accrue to other members from their attendance? Often, people attend a meeting with little intention of contributing to its business, but simply to gather information and be seen to attend. The mood of a meeting convened to take important decisions is usually quite different from that of a meeting which gathers merely to review matters of general interest. Write out a list of who will be present and alongside each name write a sentence describing what in your opinion that person wants from the meeting. Try to find out what happened during and after previous meetings.

It may be that the primary purpose of a meeting is not so much to take decisions as to act as a focal point for organisational loyalty. Attendance at non-executive meetings might create a bond between the individual and the institution. In these cases your contributions will be best appreciated if they are uncontroversial, flatter those present and reinforce favourable images of the organisation. If the meeting has firmer and more ambitious aims then ask yourself how and to what extent these aims were realised following previous meetings. Who initiated activities and who followed them up? What mistakes has the committee made in the past? What successes has it achieved?

Agenda analysis

Distinguish between items which simply present information and items requiring a decision. Identify the items that are likely to be boring and/or absorb large amounts of time. When you receive the agenda, write alongside each item a brief statement of its purpose and if appropriate, its implications for your own work. For 'information giving' items, list the points that you or someone else will be expected to transmit. If the item is intended to stimulate discussion without taking a decision, list the advantages and disadvantages to you of adopting a particular position on the issue. Predict the reactions of other members to the points you might raise. For decision taking items, write out the various possible outcomes to alternative courses of action and briefly list their implications for each committee member.

Unfortunately, some unscrupulous chairpeople know that committee members are liable to analyse an agenda carefully and so they fiddle the agenda by incorporating controversial matters into a blanket item such as 'chairperson's report' or 'matters arising', since this prevents committee members knowing that a controversial issue is to be raised, thus preventing them preparing an adequate response. In consequence, opposition to the chair's (carefully prepared) position on the issue is muted. Those who disagree with the chair do not have sufficient time to put together a convincing argument. If you suspect this has happened then, following receipt of the agenda, send a politely worded note to the committee secretary asking for confirmation that the issue in question will not be discussed at the meeting and suggest that it be included as an agenda item in the next meeting but one. A fair chairperson will not allow *decisions* (rather than general discussion) to ensue from important items raised by other committee members under 'any other business'.

Drafting intended remarks

Addressing a meeting is quite different from having a normal conversation with colleagues. Your conversational skills will already be well developed, but your presentational ability and the ease with which you can switch to a formal presentational style of delivery may not be well developed at all. Throughout your life you have engaged in conversation. As a child you learnt how to speak, listen and interact with peers. You became aware of other peoples' responses to your statements and how they react to the ways in which you put messages across. In meetings, however, people react differently; the rules of social intercourse change.

Self-check

What are the three steps involved in preparing for a committee meeting where you wish to comment on an agenda item?

Answer

Audience analysis, the purpose of the meeting and a breakdown of those attending. This will help you to decide on the general tone to adopt.

Agenda analysis, distinguish between items to convey information and those requiring a decision.

Drafting intended remarks, making a written note of the points you wish to make, including any justification. You may adapt your remarks in light of what other people say at the meeting but it is far easier to notate your points rather than speaking entirely off the cuff.

As you accumulate experience of meetings you become better able to communicate your thoughts to (potentially hostile) groups without much preparation. You learn to assess group feedback, to react to cues, to respond quickly and effectively to changes in group sentiment. Eventually, you will need only minimal notes. But to begin with, document comprehensively *all* your intended contributions.

The major advantage of addressing a meeting compared to other types of audience is that you do not have to say anything until the proceedings are well under way. You can judge the mood of the audience just before you speak and thus can make last minute adjustments to your (written) contributions. Against this benefit however is the fact that yours is but one of several contributions. The audience might not listen properly to your remarks and may misunderstand your position. Participants may become tired, restless and overly critical towards the end of the meeting.

When someone criticises you, look for some point of agreement with the other person's position. For example, you might state that the alternative view is correct in principle, but that your point raises an exception to the general rule — for reasons that you then proceed to explain. Or you might admit that the other party's case is a very good one, soundly constructed and presented, but go on to point out objections to or contradictions within the other person's argument.

Whenever you go into a meeting, assume that you will make a contribution. Be prepared, anticipate all the difficulties that might arise and predetermine your position on issues. If you take these points seriously, if you prepare for a meeting as diligently as you would prepare a speech to an external audience, you are not likely to encounter significant difficulties.

2
Personal Assertion

Objectives

This chapter will help you to:

- understand the positive role of personal assertion in modern business
- become more assertive in the work situation.

Activity

What does the phrase assertive behaviour mean to you?

You may associate the word assertive with aggression, hostility, where the intention is to hurt someone. It may bring to mind the idea of getting what you want, with little care as to what happens to others.

On the other hand, you may simply view it as taking positive action, taking charge in a given situation.

Try to keep an open mind as you begin to work through this chapter and review your definition at the end.

Assertive behaviour has a bad reputation with certain people because of its seeming associations with aggression. Advocates of assertion training deny the malevolence of such connections.

Aggression, they argue, is intended to hurt, injure, frighten or destroy. It is hostile and harmful and results from base motives such as deprivation, greed, fear or extreme frustration which are rarely encountered in normal business situations. *Assertion*, on the other hand, helps individuals to exercise initiative, translate ideas into action and maximise their creative potentials. Positive, decisive attitudes — 'attacking' problems, 'defeating' obstructions, 'mastering' situations — generate states of mind that alleviate feelings of inadequacy, overdependence on others and lack of self-confidence and self-determination. Personal assertiveness enables individuals to seize initiatives and translate ideas into action, with no implication of aggressive intent.

Assertiveness can be seen as an *alternative* to three other modes of behaviour — aggression, submission or avoidance of confrontation — available to individuals in potentially stressful situations. Note however that personal assertiveness does not imply any specific form of outward self-presentation. Was for instance Mahatma Gandhi any less effective in achieving his strategic objectives through adopting a modest, unassuming external disposition? Of course not! Yet few people would describe Mahatma Gandhi as having been unassertive, only that his assertiveness manifested itself in a particular sort of way. Real strength lies within the individual. It concerns personal conviction and how people *feel* about themselves.

Someone who believes not only in the correctness of a position, but also in his or her fundamental right to state that position should not experience too many internal inhibitions when putting forward a case — if you feel you possess the right to express yourself forcefully, you expect others to take seriously what you have to say. Importantly, mistakes and minor failures, passing anxieties and petty personal inadequacies, do not assume momentous significance in your mind. Thus, you will not worry too much if on occasion you perform inadequately and if you fail you will want to try again. A further benefit is greater empathy, respect and genuine concern for others — inward strength is usually accompanied by heightened awareness of the feelings of fellow human beings, since assertive attitudes equip individuals not only with the internal sense of security necessary for assertive action but also with an unselfish outlook and greater consideration for colleagues.

Timidity

Everyone — yes, everyone — is assertive *some* of the time, but there are major differences in *when* various people act assertively. If you suffer from timidity you need to convince yourself that you possess fundamental 'personal rights'. As a manager, you have the *right* to issue instructions and have them carried out, you have the *right* to express forcefully your own point of view and have it taken seriously and other people should listen carefully to what you say (though you must recognise that they are entitled to disagree). You have the right to initiate activity, to achieve and, importantly, to make reasonable mistakes, occasionally fail, but nevertheless try again. Why shouldn't you feel uncomfortable from time to time? Anxiety indicates your genuine concern for completing the task — you are fully entitled not to know everything about the job when you first begin and need to learn by experience.

Try to adopt an identifiable position on all important issues, but be ready to change your mind if circumstances alter or new facts emerge. Having a definite position provides an anchor for the expression of your opinions — it helps prevent the meandering of your thoughts and the enunciation of ambivalent views. Criticism by others then assumes a positive, constructive purpose since it helps you evaluate the validity of your views. Personal assertion is not emotionally selfish: you are not demanding anything you are not prepared to repay, you simply recognise an emotional self-interest in the social interactions that affect *you*.

If you were brought up as a peaceful, cooperative, generous and considerate person, you may feel uneasy about imposing your will on others, yet there is an enormous difference between emotional generosity on the one hand and self-demeaning, self-derogatory, excessively apologetic behaviour on the other. Recognise that timidity is a *learned* response, that parents, teachers and society in general expect certain people to act unassertively. Since timidity is learned then given some effort it can be monitored and controlled and previously acquired inabilities to speak and behave assertively may be overcome.

Fear

Fear is a natural physiological reaction to external threat; it warns the individual to get away from potentially damaging situations and even the *prospect* of humiliation through not being able to present oneself effectively is sufficient to induce a fearful response. Accept that you will *not* be calm and serene in every emotionally disturbing situation. Note equally however that you can learn to overcome the worst manifestations of fear (trembling, quivering voice, feeling sick, mental blocks etc). People and events are frightening only to the extent you perceive them as such, so whenever you feel afraid ask yourself the following questions:

- am I likely to be physically or mentally hurt by this situation? (If you are, then immediately withdraw)
- will I or my department suffer financially? If the scale of possible loss is so large that it causes you anxiety you should discuss the matter with colleagues
- what will happen if I take the wrong decision? Remember that you learn by making mistakes, and that you have the right to err on occasion. But if the adverse consequences of an incorrect decision will be so catastrophic that you fear taking it then pause, consider alternative procedures for taking the decision (for example, by a vote of those likely to be affected by the outcome) and if then you conclude that the decision is necessarily yours alone then accept that, provided you *do your best* and are seen to be doing your best, you have every right to fail!

The *totally* passive person is extremely rare, since life is extremely difficult without occasional personal assertion. Attitudes towards authority are important here. You need to define a personal 'space' into which other people, regardless of rank, are not allowed to intrude. Thus, for example, a superior at work is perfectly entitled to point out an inadequacy in your performance but not to interfere in your private life.

Self-check

Fear and timidity can impinge on one's ability to act in an assertive way. How can fear and timidity be overcome?

Answer
Timid people need to convince themselves that they have the right and authority to take a given course of action. Others must respect their views, even if they do not agree with them.

Most people fear failure and the consequences of taking the wrong decision, so much so that some refuse to take any decision.

Given time and experience, most people learn to control their fears and anxieties. However, in extreme cases expert help may be needed.

The moral issue

There is, perhaps, a natural tendency for people to obey institutional commands, because the survival of human society depends ultimately on rules, imposed hierarchies and the obedience of lower to upper social strata. In consequence, certain high ranking individuals can exercise assertive, even aggressive, behaviour with impunity.[1] Ruling elites become accustomed to acting assertively and being obeyed, while those who occupy lowly positions come to feel apprehensive about behaving in assertive ways. An assertive act performed by a social superior is usually considered normal and proper, whereas assertion in low status individuals can be regarded as provocative and extraordinary — it might induce in high ranking people feelings of discomfort (even resentment) and could lead to retaliation.

Without doubt, wealthy, powerful or occupationally successful people are more likely to behave assertively than others. Why is this? Is it the case that assertive people possess energy, initiative and enterprise not found in the less assertive, so that they naturally become successful, rich and powerful? Or is it simply the case that individuals who are born into or subsequently join the social elite exercise command as a matter of course and thus act assertively in fulfilment of society's expectations of how leaders ought to behave? Either argument can be used to justify assertion training. If personal assertion is associated with occupational success then assertion training may be recommended for young people expected to do well in subsequent careers. Otherwise, it might be considered useful as remedial education for those whom society expects to behave assertively, but who fail to come up to the mark in this respect. Here, personal assertiveness is seen as the *consequence*, not the cause, of privilege, wealth or success: high ranking people who are not personally assertive are considered deficient in a quality that society expects them to possess. It is no accident that educational institutions responsible for introducing young members of existing social elites to required patterns of elite social behaviour typically offer planned experience of leadership and command. Competitive sports, discipline, team activities and group ventures that require organisation and control figure prominently in their curricula. Graduates of the system should be capable of behaving assertively — anyone who isn't might be categorised as temperamentally backward and thus in need of remedial assertion training. I suspect that the raison d'etre of many (perhaps most) assertion training courses falls into this latter classification of remedial education for those an existing elite feels 'ought' to be assertive, but who are lacking in self-confidence.

The role of assertion training

Assertion training courses usually include instruction on self-awareness, body language, coping with nerves, persuasive advocacy and other aspects of verbal and non-verbal communication (voice intonation, for example), how to say no, dress and personal appearance that are relevant to influencing others. At its worst, assertion training can degenerate to a hotchpotch of disreputable techniques for coercing other people into unquestioning obedience to imposed authority. At its best it helps trainees comprehend their innermost strengths, motives and personal qualities and in consequence to apply specific assertion techniques to their daily lives without appearing unpleasant or aggressive. Courses assume that assertiveness can be taught and

Activity

To what extent do you agree with the suggestion that assertiveness is determined by the social class into which one is born?

If you are born and brought up in an environment where assertive behaviour is the expected norm, then it follows that you are more likely to act in an assertive way and be self-confident. There are still some older members of society who feel it is wrong to question the instructions of superiors. Some cultures believe it is wrong to question the actions of 'elders and betters'.

While such attitudes are breaking down, there is still an element of truth in the statement, but having said that, it is possible for any individual to benefit from assertion training.

learned and that if taught properly it will result in recipients performing more effectively in their jobs. How accurate are these claims? Is there really an educationally sound case for assertion training?

The abuse of assertion training

Usually, the extent to which a person uses assertive behaviour defines his or her location in a group's dominance hierarchy. People who occupy low status positions are usually expected to adopt modest, unassuming dispositions and thus are not considered suitable material for assertion training. In consequence, the wrong people are sometimes selected to attend courses. Individuals might be sent on courses not because of their objective training needs, but simply because they happen to occupy particular supervisory positions. Note especially how someone who is assertive but fundamentally unintelligent may, in consequence of training, become adept at coercing others, but will not be capable of developing ideas, creating new possibilities or comprehending difficult problems. Intelligent people, capable of conceptualising, exploring abstractions, absorbing and interpreting complicated information, are not necessarily assertive. They might not belong to the existing elite; they may not have received leadership experience during formative years or they might simply be unassertive by nature. Personal assertion can never act as an effective substitute for technical competence: people who are assertive but stupid have little to offer the information technology age. In its crassest and most vulgar form, assertion training will teach unscrupulous devices for dominating other people which might lead to 'survival of the fiercest' in occupational contexts but, in the absence of collateral educational development programmes, will not cause survival of the fittest for the fast moving 'high-tech' industries which increasingly dominate contemporary business affairs.

While there are undoubtedly several other factors that cause assertiveness (individual experiences, response to external attack, exposure to overtly assertive peers), strong connections do exist between assertive conduct and societal expectations of how assertively particular people should behave. Assertion training based on this principle undermines, I believe, its educational potential. It is a selfish rationalisation, implying the exploitation — emotional, financial or physical — of some people by others. There are, I suggest, good justifications for training quite distinct from this.

The case for assertion training

In principle at least, our educational values rest on notions of disciplined scepticism: questioning, probing, critical analysis, cross-examination and refusal to accept anything at face value. Progress, according to this view, results from confronting existing opinions, initiating new methods and constantly rearranging, restructuring and manipulating the outside world — *making* things happen as well as understanding why and how life is as it is. The case for assertion training may be argued in these terms. It can be said to expedite progress through stimulating initiative, enterprise and thirst for action. The brightest, keenest, most creatively energetic person will not function effectively if he or she is unable to speak confidently before others, express forthright opinions, or bring other people around to a particular point of view. Lack of self-confidence imposes enormous constraints on individual initiative. Suppression of the ego, passive acceptance of the status quo and turning inwards on oneself can thwart enterprise and creative activity. A quivering voice, repeated mental blockages, trembling or any other manifestation of excessive fear while putting forward a case will prevent individuals convincing others of the worth of their ideas.

Assertion training which focuses on awareness of innate personal rights, self-trust and awareness of latent potential helps the trainee acquire inner self-confidence and a perception of personal worth which hopefully will lead to calm in action where interpersonal relations are concerned.

Equal opportunities considerations

Parents can and frequently do rear their male and female offspring differently. They might believe in the existence of fundamental physiological sex differences that affect aggression and/or they might expect males to attain more in adult life and hence encourage personal assertion more in boys than in girls on the assumption that assertive behaviour is associated with occupational success. Achievement in competitive sports, for example, might be more highly valued in young males. Aggressive acts, fighting, displays of temper, destructive behaviour, while frowned upon in principle may in fact be tolerated in boys, but suppressed in girls.

The case for assertion training for women and girls can be built on these arguments. Boys whose aggressive acts are tolerated will come to realise they can get their own way through behaving aggressively. Violent aggression, moreover, may be followed by the victims' compliance with the aggressor's will. Eventually, aggressive acts which cause pain and distress to others might become satisfying in themselves because they are 'rewarded' by the acquiescence of others. To the extent that aggression is tolerated in boys but not in girls each sex will grow up behaving, and feeling, differently. Boys, according to this argument, will be 'naturally' assertive whereas girls will grow up 'naturally' reticent because girls, indeed any child not

---

Self-check

Identify two points in favour of assertion training and two points against.

Answer
Points against might include wrong individuals being selected for training; teaching unscrupulous devices for dominating others; 'survival of the fittest' mentality.

Points for might include improving self-confidence; helping to overcome manifestations of fear such as trembling and mental blocks; bringing out latent potential; giving individuals a feeling of self-worth; teaching skills needed in dealing with people.

---

allowed to indulge in aggressive acts, will learn to be wary of other children whose aggression is condoned.

A contrasting approach suggests that even if males and females have differing childhood experiences this does not necessarily imply that women become inwardly less assertive, only that some female attitudes towards leadership and control are essentially different to those found in men. A woman might feel inwardly self-confident, but present herself in ways that make her appear to men as lacking in assertion. The over-whelming majority of high-ranking employees in industry, commerce, the professions (including teaching) and the public service are men. Thus, males will in the main be responsible for monitoring and appraising the performances of female juniors. Inevitably, men will bring to their evaluations masculine norms, values, attitudes and perspectives. A male superior might misinterpret the behaviour of a female subordinate and classify her (wrongly) as unassertive. Then, remedial assertion training might be recommended to enable her to overcome this 'deficiency'. In consequence, it becomes a device for encourag-ing women to behave 'as if' they were men. Women are taught to ape masculine forms of assertive behaviour. Assertion training — on this interpretation — is a fundamentally sexist activity, requiring females to sacrifice their essential identities as women.

Without doubt, childhood experiences can and do repress

initiative and the desire for involvement in organised hierarchical activities. An able woman capable of clear, incisive rational thought may not be equally capable of coherent, uninhibited expression. Assertion training, hopefully, will convince an excessively introverted woman of her right to exhibit positive behaviour and express herself openly, honestly, persuasively and in a forceful manner. She will be better able to mix easily with colleagues of either sex and differing backgrounds. Women's assertion training can legitimately be regarded as recognition of the adverse effects of unfair discriminatory childrearing practices and societal attitudes that can and sometimes do conspire to make women less assertive than men.

There are, then, many problems associated with assertion training — choice of participants, ethicality of aims and objectives, choice of technique, single versus mixed-sex courses and so on. I conclude nevertheless that assertion training, properly interpreted and skilfully applied, can be justified against sound educational criteria and that training can represent a valuable addition to a vocational training programme, though too often it is popular for the wrong reasons. Individuals selected for training should be chosen because of their particular training needs, not because of the supervisory positions they happen to occupy and it should never be used to convey techniques and devices for extracting unquestioning obedience from other people. Assertion training should not be offered as a substitute for other training activities. Some people may be made worse, not better, by it.

Becoming more assertive

Initially, select only straightforward social situations for practising assertion skills (a routine meeting with colleagues for instance) since then you will be able to observe the effects of your new found assertive behaviour and quickly withdraw without causing offence if you make a mistake. Make a mental note of how others respond to various forms of assertive behaviour and analyse their responses. Expect to make slow progress at first — seek gradually to build up a personal inventory of assertive skills. The following activities may be practised in suitable circumstances.

Saying 'no'

Supervisors must sometimes refuse requests from other people. It is not always easy to say no firmly and clearly, yet not create offence. We all know *how* to say no, *when* we ought to say no and *why* certain requests cannot be accepted, but too often we end up agreeing to an unreasonable request instead of rejecting the proposition. If you believe you should refuse a particular request, ask yourself the following questions:

- what consequences will result from the refusal?
- how will the other person feel about the rejection, are those feelings justified and do they matter?
- what are the costs and benefits of the refusal to you and to the other person?
- what are your *real* motives for refusing the request? Are they selfish, or in the best interests of the work of your department?

Saying yes when you should say no may lead to a quiet life in the short term, but can eventually result in disruption. Your apparent friendliness and willingness to cooperate might encourage unreasonable demands from others. You are, of course, at a disadvantage because the person making a request has time to prepare his or her approach and devise a strategy for asking the question.

Identify the *purpose* of the request as well as the required action and try to empathise with the feelings of the other party. If you have to refuse, preface your refusal with a remark such as, 'I know you feel strongly about . . ., but I'm afraid I'm really not in a position to be able to . . ., because . . . (give reasons)' and if possible, offer a compromise. Do not allow yourself to be side-tracked: if the conversation begins to meander then restate your initial refusal but with a different choice of words. Aim to be pleasant and recognise that saying no does not necessarily imply dislike of the other person or necessarily earn the animosity of that individual. It is not a crime to refuse a request and you have every *right* to reject unreasonable demands.

Using body language

Observe carefully the effects of your gestures on other people. Vary the gestures you use and record the response. Try occasionally to smile in situations where you would not normally do so and assess afterwards whether the smile improved or worsened the efficiency of the interaction. Note the importance of the physical proximity of the person you are addressing in defining the character of your personal relationship. Feelings about others can change dramatically as their physical distance alters, particularly as they draw close.

Direct eye contact is useful when arguing with someone, since it reinforces the firmness of your views. A steady gaze can indicate a solid inner conviction and you should always look at people when saying no. Note also that eye contact indicates the degree of interest shown by one person in the conversation of another. If you are bored, irritated, embarrassed by a conversation or fearful of the person you are addressing you are unlikely to look for long periods into his or her eyes. However, take care when experimenting with eye contact — it makes you appear assertive, but murders have been committed on account of misinterpreted stares.

Dealing with abuse

Never cooperate with abuse but do not respond aggressively. As far as possible, anticipate and prepare for hostile criticism. Avoid sarcasm and look instead for the basic motive underlying the abuse, then devise a positive strategy for overcoming the implied criticism. Is the matter personal, or is it an *issue* that is under attack? Are there any reasonable points in the other party's statement? If there are, agree with them and hence establish a common ground. Avoid answering abuse with further abuse.

The overbearing manager

Some executives become bullies. They get so used to having their own way that they interpret queries as insubordination and the exercise of independent initiative as the deliberate sabotage of their work. Because they are never answered back, they become pompous, conceited and insensitive to the feelings of subordinates.

Anger and self-control

Anger is caused by and arises within the individual. Unfortunate external events do not necessarily make a person angry, only the way in which they are perceived. Everyone feels angry occasionally. Supervisors, unfortunately, sometimes vent their anger on employees who cannot answer back and hence never realise how angry they actually become. The absence of fair, constructive criticism can cause individuals to believe that they are always right and that their feelings and demands are *always* justified. Thus, anger results when a desire is converted into a *demand*, and the demand is rejected by another person. You do not become angry just because a wish is not satisfied (otherwise you would be angry all the time), yet you might be furious if an *entitlement* is not realised. Hence, a good way to begin to overcome anger is to ask yourself whether it is reasonable for you to demand that the thing causing your anger be completed, since if you demand nothing you will never be disappointed.

Paradoxically, people who lose their temper most often are frequently those who most lack the skills of personal assertion. They cope with (perceived) threats aggressively rather than in less injurious ways.

Activity

When was the last time you lost your temper at work?

Try to identify the circumstances and cause/s. If you are unable to recollect events, try to conduct the analysis the next time you lose your temper at work.

We all have to learn to control our behaviour. In many instances, it is a trivial matter that causes an individual to lose his or her temper and loss of control is more likely to occur when one is tired or working under stress.

If you are prone to aggressive outbursts then you need to learn how to relax, converse and listen. It is up to *you* to control your behaviour: you choose the clothes you put on every morning — you must similarly learn how to choose appropriate emotional reactions to various stressful and anger inducing situations. Keep an 'anger diary' detailing all the incidents that cause you to feel angry. List everything — embarrassment at being looked at, unfulfilled promises, disappointments, arguments, complaints by colleagues etc — no matter how trivial they might at first appear. Specify how you felt before, during and after each incident. A picture will soon emerge of the types of situation that make you angry and how you react to them.

Note

1. The argument here is that the social order, ultimately, is maintained by violence. There are police, riot squads, armed militia etc to enforce societal rules on those reluctant to obey. Ruling elites decide the institutional guidelines, social norms and cultural values that society imposes on its members. It follows that social elites are necessarily involved in aggression — albeit vicarious — towards some non-conformist groups.

3
Effective Communication

Objectives

This chapter will help you to:

- become a more effective communicator
- select an appropriate communication medium in a given situation.

To be an effective supervisory manager you must be good at communication. Your credibility as group leader, facilitator and organiser depends substantially on how clearly and forcefully you can express your views. A badly written letter or memorandum, an ill-considered or poorly presented report or even an incoherent statement over the telephone can create damaging impressions of your competence. Communication involves the exchange of information, opinion and sentiment. You need to communicate in order to expedite the work of your department, to motivate, inform, deal with grievances, liaise with outsiders and coordinate your team. This chapter will outline the basic notions of communication and briefly describe the common communication techniques: memoranda, letters, written reports and meetings of staff.

What is communication?

Communication involves the initiation, transfer, reception and interpretation of information. Messages might be orders,

---

Activity

How effective are you as a communicator? Try to identify two occasions when subordinates have failed to act or misunderstood a communication from you. What, in your opinion, went wrong?

It is too simplistic to imagine that failure of subordinates to carry out your instructions can have nothing to do with the communication itself. Messages may be perfectly clear to the sender but misunderstood by the receiver. Care needs to be taken in selecting the most appropriate medium, language etc.

In identifying what went wrong you have probably referred to what communication theory calls 'barriers'. Compare your points with those mentioned in the next section.

---

recommendations, explanations or simple statements of fact. They are encoded via a particular communication medium (ie you choose an appropriate form of words and means for their transmission), and the message is sent, received and acted upon by the other party. Unfortunately, the process of encoding (and decoding) messages is liable to distortion, and several barriers to effective communication exist.

The *medium* of communication used — the letter, memo, report or whatever, is the link between transmitter and receiver. Both need to 'tune-in' to the medium. You must therefore select a medium suited to the needs of the transmittee. Just as a radio signal must transmit on the same wavelength as receiving units, so a supervisor must choose language and presentational techniques appropriate for the audiences for which messages are intended. Successful communication results in recipients *understanding* messages, which requires recipients to interpret the words, body language (where appropriate), hints and implications contained within the messages sent. There are several barriers to communication, which include the following.

Noise

This is the term used to describe interference with signals. In verbal communication noise can involve bad habits of speech (mumbling, cliché ridden conversation, wandering off the subject etc). For written messages, noise arises from imprecise description, confused and illogical argument, poor grammar, bad layout and inconsistent paragraph structure.

Excessively long chains of command

In large organisations, messages might need to pass through so many intermediate levels of authority that their meanings are lost. Each recipient at each level must interpret and transmit the message. Information that is not immediately useful to a recipient might be ignored or its relay held up for long periods.

Communication overload

Individuals might receive so many messages that most are disregarded. In consequence, arbitrary decisions are taken regarding which messages to act upon and which to ignore.

Inappropriate message construction

A well written, concise memorandum might please its originator, but fail through being written in language 'over the head' of the recipient. When constructing messages, you need to consider the intended audience; what is simple to one person can be unintelligible to another. In particular, technical communications need to be semantically precise. Generally, short and simple words and phrases are preferable; technical 'jargon' should be avoided. Note however that 'redundancy' of information — saying the same thing several times but in different words — does have a positive role in technical communication. Redundancy reinforces major points and assists the absorption of complex messages.

Inability to listen

Too often, we see what we want to see and hear only what we want to hear. Feedback is therefore essential to good communication. It confirms that messages have been received and understood. If the communicator is entirely insensitive to feedback, then half the communication equation ceases to exist.

Activity

As a manager, you need to understand the principles and methods of communication, and much of your success will depend on how well you communicate both with colleagues and the outside world. Think of recent occasions when people misunderstood what you said or wrote because you had not communicated your message properly. What were the causes of the problem?

Your answer might have included: excessive use of jargon, mumbling, bad grammar, people not listening, recipients of the communication already being overloaded with so many messages that most are disregarded.

Communication systems

A communications system links together the constituent parts of a firm's organisation providing for the creation, distribution and execution of instructions. Good internal communications will ensure that employees are well informed about current events and the intentions of colleagues and will encourage subordinates to gather and transmit information. Formal media for transferring messages include letters and memoranda, reports, the telephone, pamphlets, handbooks, notices and posters, as well as face to face oral communication, but informal channels are also important. In particular, the so called 'grapevine' can be a primary medium for the distribution of information. This is an unofficial, loose collection of communication passages that circumvent and sometimes even replace orthodox communication procedures. Grapevines are common where employees know each other well and exchange information casually without the knowledge or permission of higher authority. They are particularly virulent when senior management deliberately withholds information affecting employees' welfare. Hence, rumours concerning possible redundancies, confidential personal matters, gossip or scandal will be quickly and widely dispersed through the grapevine system. Although the grapevine is strictly unofficial, people holding key positions within it (namely those who spread the most information) often find their status in the official system enhanced through grapevine activities.

The most efficient way of suppressing a grapevine is for management to present clear, accurate and comprehensive information to employees, yet management may decide to allow a grapevine to survive because it provides a fast and effective means of distributing news. Also, views which management might not want to be made known officially can be disseminated through the grapevine. The obvious disadvantages of the grapevine system are its tendency to distort reality and its potential for malicious initiation of unsavoury rumours. Even without deliberate malice, grapevines frequently misrepresent issues since the facts behind situations tend to be exaggerated or otherwise altered at each stage in the dissemination process. There is no mechanism for checking the validity of the information transmitted or for refuting falsehoods.

Supervisors are expected both to manage the official communications system and to be heavily involved in the grapevine. You need to be able to issue written instructions, brief a team of subordinates, write letters, memoranda and reports.

Activity

In your own organisation, is there any conflict between official communication channels and the 'grapevine'? What is the policy of senior management with regard to disseminating information to all levels of staff?

It is amazing, and perhaps a little worrying, how much attention staff pay to information coming through the unofficial grapevine. News concerning retirements, new appointments, sackings etc often circulates along the grapevine long before the official announcement. Where senior management operate a more open policy on keeping lower levels of staff informed, the grapevine ceases to be as important.

Management by walking around (MBWA)

Listening and talking to employees on an informal basis in workplace situations is perhaps the best communication device available to the management of a firm. MBWA involves gathering information, assessing morale, and generally learning how people feel about the organisation and each other. Managers discover which jobs are easy and which difficult, and observe directly the quality and productivity problems experienced by workers. Advantages to the practice are that it demonstrates management's commitment to good employee communication, and provides valuable feedback on the operational effectiveness of policy decisions. Disadvantages are that it absorbs large amounts of management time (possibly with few tangible outputs), that workers may learn how to manipulate the system (by predicting when managers are likely to pay a visit and then appearing to be working harder than is actually the case), and that managers might engage in MBWA simply to waste time.

Writing instructions

When writing instructions you have to describe, explain and/or specify quantities or relations. You do not normally have to evaluate, justify, persuade or recommend (as you would in some other forms of written communication — reports for instance). It is essential that subordinates *understand* your instructions, but they need not remember them, because in implementing the instructions they can refer to the document you have prepared. Thus, you do not have to repeat points to ensure they are memorised but you must provide foolproof procedures for getting things done. Clarity of exposition and logical *ordering* of material are thus fundamentally important here.

The introduction to your document should describe the equipment or system to be operated, explaining its purpose, why it is needed and providing an overall context for its use. Specific instructions are normally prefaced by an action: 'Unscrew the top from the bottle', 'Take a piece of metal four inches long', 'Carefully remove the contents' etc. Ask yourself the following questions.

Who will use the instructions?

Never assume that people reading your instructions are as competent and motivated as yourself. There is nothing wrong in 'talking down' to the reader (within reason) if by so doing you clarify the exposition. Instructions must be clear, complete, concise and simple, but an instruction that is clear to one person might confuse someone else. Try therefore to predict every conceivable question that a reader might ask and incorporate the answers into your text. The more varied the readership the greater the detail with which you need to describe each aspect of the instructions.

How knowledgeable is the reader?

In choosing an appropriate style of presentation and vocabulary, consider the backgrounds, knowledge and experience of potential users of the instructions. Do not use technical terms that will not be familiar to the typical reader and always choose the lowest common denominator for your model. An expert reader will find much of the material presented to be superfluous but the expert will forgive you and no harm is done. Conversely, an inexperienced novice may find brief instructions which assume prior knowledge or experience to be incomprehensible. If potential readers are drawn from diverse backgrounds then you might need to draft several different sets of instructions explaining the same thing in different ways depending on the likely knowledgeability of the intended reader.

What do you want the reader to be able to do?

Define precisely a successful outcome to the operation. List all the materials and other resources needed and list *all* the things that could go wrong. How quickly should the reader be able to complete the operation? Is it necessary for the reader to understand the thing before operating it? For instance, you do not need to *understand* how a petrol engine works in order to change a spark plug but you cannot fine tune an engine without knowing something about how engines work.

There are certain rules for writing instructions:

- arrange the instructions in the exact order in which operations should be completed

- write each instruction in the simplest language possible
- be comprehensive. Ensure that all necessary steps are included. Do not assume that readers will themselves be able to fill in missing sections. Readers will not be annoyed if you write too much — they will simply skip through what to them is superfluous information. Spell out every detail that could cause doubt
- write in the imperative (as in this list). Avoid abbreviations, and use complete sentences rather than instructions written in note form
- set out the information in the form of a list, like this one, with each instruction clearly labelled. Use plenty of headings. Key words may be typed in capital letters
- avoid ambiguous words. Ambiguity might arise through words having meaning *relative* to a position (for example, the 'left' of this page could mean the left as you look at it, or its own left as it lies on the table); or through words having double meanings (the word 'replace' could mean either 'refit the existing' or 'fit a new part') and avoid using unfamiliar words that some readers might not understand. Few readers will bother looking up the correct meaning in a dictionary, so some might misinterpret words
- at the end of the list of instructions, insert a checklist of things to look for if the operation has gone wrong. A brief summary of the *major* steps might also be useful.

Finally, get someone who has not previously performed the task to work through the instructions, without help from anyone. Then get a second person to do the same. Revise your instructions in the light of what goes wrong. Once the final version has been circulated, check periodically to ensure the instructions are actually understood.

Writing a letter

Most people in business would claim to be able to write a letter, yet when one reads many of the business letters one receives, often from high ranking officials within firms, it is soon obvious that this is not so. The problem, I believe, is that

---

Activity

Look out a selection of business letters that you have written recently and cast a critical eye over them. Can you identify any faults with your style or layout? We can all fall into the trap of churning out letters, using a basic layout and form of words irrespective of the context.

---

letter writers unconsciously create two categories of letter: those regarded as 'important' and which in consequence they consider carefully and redraft several times and those classified as 'routine', which are drafted just once — typically towards the end of a tiring day — without much thought and which, stylistically, leave much to be desired. To improve the quality of your routine letter writing you should adopt certain predetermined rules. Start by jotting down — in the order they occur to you — the points you wish to make. Think of the reader. How do you want and expect the reader to react to the letter?

Much of the impression you create will depend on the *organisation* of the letter — the ordering, layout and tone of its presentation — so arrange your list of points into a new and more logical order. Have a subject heading at the top and go straight to the point of the letter in the first paragraph. The current convention when replying to a letter from someone else is to begin with the words, 'Thank you for your letter of . . . (date) . . . concerning . . . (details of subject)', followed by further information on the matters discussed. If you are initiating correspondence, state at the outset the information you need to transmit or require from the other party. Four sections are needed: information, starting with the most important point; supporting details, evidence and views; a summary stating your conclusions and the actions that need to follow; and the closure, thanking the reader for his or her attention and looking forward to a reply. If there are enclosures to accompany the letter, list them after your signature.

Aim for a simple and direct style. Be as clear and concise as you can. Avoid pompous phrases or anything hinting of intimidation. You need to connect with the reader and invoke in that person an empathetic response. When you conduct a verbal conversation, you supplement your spoken words with gestures, facial expressions and body movements that indicate the emotional context of your remarks. In a letter, however, you have none of these supplementary means of communication. The tone of the letter is the sole indication of your state of mind during its composition. Thus, you must choose your words carefully and constantly check to ensure they will not cause offence. If a letter is more than two pages long it is possibly better to rewrite it as a report (see below) to be sent accompanied by a short covering letter.

Memoranda

Memoranda are used instead of letters for interdepartmental communication within organisations. They are usually shorter and more direct than letters. There is no need for a salutation ('Dear Sir') at the start or 'Yours faithfully' at the finish. Otherwise, memos should be structured in the same order as letters. Avoid long sentences, use plenty of headings and subheadings and number the points so that recipients can refer to relevant details in their replies. A memorandum is better than a telephone call in that it provides a permanent record of the communication (memos should always be signed, or at least initialled). The disadvantage of their use, however, lies in the tendency of many managers to write too many memoranda and to distribute copies of each to people with only marginal interest in the content.

Activity

Collect two reports recently prepared within your organisation. Examine their style, layout, clarity, the usefulness of the information presented, the suitability for the target audience of the language used, and the frequency and helpfulness of headings within the text.

Reports

Reports are a widely used method of collecting and transmitting information for management control. They can be written by specialists, widely circulated and studied at convenient times. A report is a presentation of facts, opinions and recommendations for action. Information contained in a report should be concise, accurate and logically organised. The precise structure of a report will depend on its purpose, but all reports should contain statements of their terms of reference and brief summaries of major conclusions. All report writing involves the following tasks.

Collection of material

Obtaining information, conducting research, checking the accuracy of facts, distinguishing facts from opinions.

Selection of material

Isolating important material, deciding which facts to use in support of arguments.

Ordering sections

Classification of material, placing sections in a logical order, deciding headings and sub-headings.

Writing the report

Choosing a style appropriate to the audience for which the report is intended, choice of illustrations, tables, graphs and diagrams.

Presentation

There is no single correct way in which to structure a report. Here is one possible layout:

    title page
    summary
    table of contents
    introduction
    text of main body of the report
    conclusions
    recommendations

appendices containing tables, technical calculations, references etc.

The first thing to consider is 'for whom' the report is intended and what you hope it will achieve. Unfortunately, some managers have split personalities where report writing is concerned. They write in pompous language they would never otherwise use. The style of a report should aim to *inform* rather than impress. It should be clear, concise and comprehensive. Here are some guidelines for writing reports.

- put the title (which should fully describe the contents of the report), together with your name, departmental address, date of submission and circulation list on a separate covering page
- begin the report with a one or two paragraph summary of its major findings. For long reports, have a contents page with page references to sections
- start the introduction with a clear statement of why the report is necessary and its terms of reference. Outline previous investigations undertaken on the same subject then state the objectives of the present report. Terms of reference are extremely important: a 'report on office stationery' for example might involve a listing of stationery currently in use; a report on stationery theft, waste or improper utilisation; a review of procedures for stationery issue; investigation of stationery procurement methods and so on. Thus, your report should begin with a *precise* definition of its contents sufficiently detailed to inform readers whether the information is relevant to their particular needs
- in writing the body of the report, put yourself in the position of the eventual reader, asking what he or she needs to know, what sort of illustrations, examples and supplementary data will help the reader understand the discussion and what background knowledge the reader already possesses
- keep within your terms of reference. Check the relevance of each paragraph against your central thesis and arrange the material in order of importance *from the reader's point of view*. State the fundamental points first; the

detail later — readers find assimilation of detail easier if they have been given a general framework into which it can be fitted.

Editing a report

Adopt the following procedure for editing a report.

- Ensure that all the sentences make sense and have commas and full stops in the correct places.
- Cut out redundant sentences and superfluous words within sentences.
- Check that you have not started successive sentences or paragraphs with the same word (especially 'the').
- Look for excessive repetition of the same word within a page. Use alternatives where a word appears too often.
- Compare the introduction with the conclusion or recommendations. Have you completed everything you set out to do?
- Make sure that the headings and sub-headings follow a logical order.

Activity

To what extent does your organisation use committees and meetings as a medium of communication?

List the committees on which you serve, identifying the purpose of each. In the next section, the main types of committee are identified. Try to slot your committees into the categories mentioned.

Meetings and committees

Meetings are a primary medium of communication within organisations. Most involve 'committees', which are groups of people to which issues are referred for consideration, investigation or resolution.

Committees differ from other groups in the *formality* of their processes. They have a chairperson and secretary; their terms of reference are predetermined; and work follows a pre-set agenda.

Rules of procedure

These may be established by convention or, for formal committees, embodied in a document called the *standing orders* of the committee. Before becoming heavily involved in committee work (which is inevitable as your career develops) you need to be familiar with the bureaucracy and protocol of meetings, but you should also realise that behind formal structures lie a number of practical demands. Agendas *must* be completed, all members must be allowed to speak and efficient mechanisms for fairly resolving internal disagreements are required.

First, someone must convene the meeting. This means informing all committee members of the time and location, booking a room (and arranging for it to be tidied up after the meeting), ensuring there will be enough chairs and tables and that someone will take minutes, and circulating the agenda. Members should previously have been invited to submit items for inclusion on the agenda and meetings should not be convened on dates or at times when key members cannot attend. Usually, meetings are convened by a committee secretary who, as well as taking minutes, will keep copies of past minutes, membership lists, copies of standing orders etc. If the secretary is a permanent committee member while the chair is an elected position then the secretary might temporarily chair the committee while elections take place. The treasurer of a committee deals with its finances and presents financial reports. Nominations for elected officers require a proposer and a seconder and may occur either in advance of or during the meeting. Postal and/or proxy votes may or may not be allowed depending on the committee's rules.

Co-opted members serve only for temporary periods. They might replace absent members or provide specialist help. Co-opted membership ceases when the committee is re-elected unless that person is elected to serve for a further term. A coopted member may vote, whereas 'consultant' members, who only participate for part of a meeting, may not. Any member can propose a motion for debate. Once a motion is accepted it becomes a 'resolution' of the committee. Subcommittees may be established to deal with routine or highly specialist matters. They report to the main committee and *recommend* rather than take direct action.

Formal committees

In formal meetings (Company Annual General Meetings or Local Authority committees, for example), certain bureaucratic procedures must be followed.

The quorum of a committee (ie the minimum number of people who must be present before a meeting can take place) may be determined at its first meeting. If a meeting is inquorate it is still possible to discuss issues, but no decisions may be taken. If a member notices an irregularity in procedure (eg if the chair has failed to notice that the meeting is inquorate) or in the behaviour of another member then he or she may raise a *point of order*, which may be put to the chair at any time and must be considered at once. The chair decides whether the challenge is to be accepted. If something is not in order then it must be remedied straightaway, otherwise the meeting continues as before. If the chair overrules a point of order then the person who raised it might challenge the decision in the form of a motion, which must be seconded. The chair then states the question and a vote is taken on whether to sustain or overrule the chair. Should this result in a tie, the chair is sustained. A point of information can be raised at any time, subject to permission of the speaker. The member wishing to interrupt should put the point to the chair, who then asks the speaker if he or she is willing to accept it (there is no obligation to do so). If accepted, the point is made and the speaker comments on the matter before proceeding.

A motion needs a proposer and a seconder. Usually, these individuals speak in favour of the motion, one after the other, followed by two speakers against the motion. Debate then ensues, with the chair selecting who shall speak. If the proposed motion is one of 'no confidence' in the chair, then someone else (perhaps the secretary) takes the chair during discussions of and

Self-check

Explain the following terms used in connection with meetings:

— quorum
— coopted member
— agenda.

Answer

Quorum: the minimum number of people who must be present before any decisions can be voted upon.

Co-opted member: an individual serving on a committee who has not been elected. He/she may be representing an absent elected member or be providing specialist help. The coopted member may vote at the meeting.

Agenda: a list of the items to be discussed at a particular meeting. It usually follows a standard format.

the vote on this issue. Matters become complicated when amendments to motions are proposed. The first motion that is brought forward is called the 'original motion'. Amendments are motions which seek to alter or improve an original motion. If the proposed alteration would destroy the original motion it might be referred to as a 'wrecking amendment': many chairpeople refuse to allow the proposal of wrecking amendments, on the grounds that the proper way to destroy a motion is to vote against it. Once an amendment has been accepted the amended motion is known as the 'substantive motion' and it replaces the original motion. This substantive motion might consist of the original motion with words added or deleted or have counter-proposals in place of those initially intended. Amendments themselves can be amended, and great confusion can ensue. Each amendment is taken one at a time, each must be proposed and seconded and if the proposer wishes to withdraw the amendment the seconder must be asked whether he or she is willing to allow this to occur. Commonsense is needed when amending motions. If the discussion becomes immersed in amendments it might be better to terminate the debate and start again from a new original motion (though committee work purists might disagree with me here).

A discussion might wind itself up naturally, without need for intervention from the chair, or a separate motion could be proposed that the motion under debate be now voted upon, or a 'guillotine' (ie a time limit on discussion of a particular topic) might be applied. Unless the debate has raised supplementary issues that require an adjournment to allow members to think over the issues at greater length, a vote is taken and the meeting moves to the next agenda item.

Advantages of the committee system

Committees are the most popular vehicle for taking important decisions in industry and commerce. They have several advantages:

- increased communications between people and departments leading to easier coordination and management control
- utilisation of the talents, experience and creative abilities of several people. An individual might not recognise some key element in a problem, or be aware of all potential solutions
- shared responsibility for decisions. No one person has to bear sole liability for mistakes
- extensive discussion of issues and the generation of fresh ideas. Problems can be examined in depth. Opposing views will emerge, consideration of which should improve the quality of final decisions
- compromises between conflicting positions will have to be reached. Hence, arbitrary or extreme decisions can be avoided
- representatives from many interest groups can take part in organisational decision making. In principle, this should encourage acceptance of joint decisions by all who are involved in the decision taking process. Participation should raise enthusiasm for the implementation of the decisions
- avoidance of the concentration of power into small

numbers of hands. Individuals are required to justify their intentions before colleagues, who may challenge the views expressed.

Disadvantages of the committee system

Although widely used, committees need not be the best medium for taking decisions. Indeed, cynics describe committees as comprising of 'the unfit, selected by the unwilling, to do the unnecessary' and without doubt procedures that rely solely on individual authority can be extremely effective. Problems faced by committees include the following.

High operating costs

Typically, committee members are highly paid managers whose time could profitably be spent elsewhere. The wage cost of a committee of, say, 10 people meeting for half a day, is substantial. Decisions taken by individuals require only one person's time.

Discussion of trivial issues

Each committee member has a right to express opinions and to cross-examine and challenge the views of other participants. Sometimes, members reiterate sentiments that have already been expressed in slightly different forms. Personal conflicts can develop, arguments might be tedious, long winded and add little to the quality of debate.

Indecision

Unanimity of opinion within a committee is rare. Were participants to agree on all issues there would be little need for the committee; decisions reflecting members' views could be taken by a single representative. Committee decisions, therefore, are usually compromises which do not fully satisfy any interested party. More positive courses of action may be preferable. The problem is acute in committees which require unanimous agreement for decisions rather than a simple majority vote. Here, minority groups hold great power. They can hold up a committee's work through withholding their consent to particular proposals.

This tendency to indecision can lead to one or a few members assuming disproportionately influential roles. Anyone who repeatedly offers definite middle-of-the-road solutions may quickly assume a position of leadership. Other members follow dominant participants not because they agree with their views, but merely to avoid stalemate and interminable discussion.

Abrogation of individual responsibility

Collective decisions do not require individuals to assume personal responsibility for mistakes, thus it is hard to identify blameworthy staff. Guilty parties can hide behind the ambiguities created by joint decision making; it is difficult to investigate how a bad decision came to be taken within a particular committee.

Slow decision making

The larger the committee and the more it discusses issues, the longer it takes to reach decisions. Some important items on meeting agendas might not be dealt with in the time allowed and so may be held over until the next scheduled meeting. Exceptionally difficult problems are often referred to subcommittees, so increasing the delay in reaching final decisions.

Committees operate within normal line, staff or functional organisation structures. Ideally, they should complement, not replace, individual executive power. In some cases, line executives initiate committees to examine problems which are beyond the limits of their personal knowledge. Otherwise committees exist permanently, their members being either appointed (by higher management), elected (by colleagues), or holding ex officio positions. To avoid subsequent disagreements about what is actually decided, all committee decisions should be minuted. Usually, the minutes of a meeting are circulated to committee members who, at the next meeting, will accept or reject them as a fair and accurate record of actual discussions.

Basic requirements

If committees are to operate successfully, a number of basic requirements should be met. Committees must:

- have definite, identifiable purposes with explicit terms of reference. The end result of a committee's work should be a clear decision, accompanied by a statement of how the decision is to be implemented, or a written report addressed to a higher level of authority. The people or departments responsible for carrying out a committee decision should be specified in the minutes of the meeting

- be of reasonable size. What constitutes a reasonable size varies depending on circumstances; precise judgements are impossible. Committees should be large enough to incorporate all relevant specialisations and people with appropriate experience, but not so large that decisions cannot be taken with speed and efficiency. A meeting of three or four people is more of a discussion between colleagues than a committee as such: there would be little point in adopting formal committee procedures (agendas, minutes, chairperson, secretary etc) in such circumstances. Numbers exceeding 15 (approximately) create problems of control and it is unlikely that all members could make significant contributions to the work of such a large group
- consist of competent people who are interested in committee work. Often, ex officio committee members care little about items under consideration and attend only for the sake of being seen. Participants with insufficient technical knowledge or who cannot put across their ideas are burdensome to the group.

Apart from possessing these positive characteristics it is important that committees should not:

- consider issues beyond their terms of reference or authority. What is the point of wasting time deliberating over matters which the committee cannot control?
- be established to deal with unimportant matters. Trivial decisions can be taken by a single executive without incurring the costs and inconvenience of committees.

A fundamental but essentially insoluble difficulty with committee work is the inequality of status of participants. For instance, a board of directors typically contains a managing director, who is the chief executive of the firm, and other full time directors who are heads of functional departments. Outside the boardroom, executive directors are subordinates of the managing director. Within the board of a public company, all directors are equal in that their primary duty is to protect the interests of the shareholders who elected them. Issues will be discussed and votes taken, but disagreement with and, ultimately, voting against the managing director, is a serious matter indeed for an individual director, since after the meeting a dissenting director reverts to the role of subordinate. Note here that ability is not necessarily related to status. The contributions of junior committee members might outweigh those of participants possessing greater status and authority within the firm.

Activity

The chair plays an important role in the work of a committee. You may have chaired meetings either at work and/or in some social/leisure activity.

Outline the duties of a chairperson.

The next section deals with how to chair a meeting and should be studied carefully. Essentially, the function of the chair is:

— to plan, liaising with the committee secretary to ensure that the agenda is prepared, notification of the meeting is circulated, minutes of the last meeting prepared etc
— to prepare for the actual meeting by familiarising yourself with the agenda, who is likely to speak etc
— to control the meeting, ensuring that speakers do not stray from the point, no arguments occur, people are given a fair chance to speak to the items on the agenda
— to put the motions to be voted upon
— generally to ensure that the meeting is conducted in a legal and fair manner.

Chairing a meeting

The fact that committee members might not interact socially outside committee meetings and the need to get things done quickly and efficiently create the requirement for a group leader in the form of a committee chairperson. This individual is the 'custodian' of the committee's rules of procedure. The ideal chairperson will recognise significant issues, encourage minorities to air their views, ensure that all aspects of a problem and its possible solutions are considered and systematically structure the debate. Chairing a committee is not easy. A chairperson needs to be competent, experienced in committee work and have his or her authority accepted by all the sectional interests involved.

If you are asked to chair a meeting, you need to do three things: plan, prepare, and perform. Planning involves having the committee secretary issue the notice of the meeting's occurrence, ensuring that administrative details (room booking etc) are dealt with and drafting an agenda with the secretary. Routine matters should appear first, more substantial matters later. Note that each significant issue should be listed as a separate agenda item. It is bad practice to conceal major and contentious matters under the blanket heading 'chairperson's report' or similar catchall item since members with views on these issues will be caught unawares, not having been given sufficient time to prepare their positions. A typical order for an agenda is as follows:

apologies for absence
agreement of the minutes of the last meeting
matters arising from the minutes
chairperson's report
other items
major items for discussion and resolution
any other business
arrangements for the next meeting.

The secretary will take minutes, recording briefly what was said and noting the decisions reached. It is essential that *all* decisions are recorded, not just some of them. Minutes should be written up immediately after the meeting (while the memory is still fresh) and circulated to participants. They must be confirmed at the next meeting as a fair and accurate record of those proceedings. Usually the chair has discretion to alter the order in which agenda items are discussed, provided the changes are announced at the beginning of the meeting.

To prepare for your duties you must familiarise yourself with all agenda items — if necessary by approaching informally the members who asked for their inclusion. You should identify the contentious items and predict who will want to speak about them and how long each item will take. Write out a list of new members (if any) who will need to be introduced to the meeting and if possible approach newcomers beforehand to brief them about how the business of the meeting will proceed. Make sure they know how to put items on the agenda and the rules of debate. Circulate background papers to members, indicating aspects of particular interest to each person and warning them if they will be expected to make presentations or special reports on specific issues.

In the performance of your duties try always to facilitate rather than lead discussion. Recognise however that you are ultimately responsible for conducting the meeting properly in accordance with standing orders or other predetermined rules. Thus, participants should address the chair, not each other and should speak only when invited to do so by the chair. Your aims are to utilise to the best advantage all the talents and experiences of participants, ensure that all interested parties have opportunities to express their views and avoid unnecessary conflicts and animosities among participants. Your specific duties include the following.

Controlling debate

As a chairperson you must ensure fair play during meetings. You must get through the agenda in good time, while enabling all participants to air their views. You call on people to speak and hurry them up when the usefulness of their contributions has been exhausted. If votes must be taken you decide when these should occur. A good chairperson is neutral between the parties but nevertheless always in control. Occasionally, you might have to tell speakers to finish their points quickly or not to digress into irrelevant areas. Aim for the maximum involvement of members. If members' contributions are not treated with respect then members will quickly stop contributing. Refer to members by name (and nameplates are useful for large meetings) and always be courteous.

Resolving disputes

Sometimes, disagreements occur not through fundamental hostilities but because issues are unclear. Try to clarify problems independently or by drawing other people into a discussion. One method is to ask everyone in attendance (assuming of course the number of participants is reasonably small) to state an opinion on an issue. Dangers arise in that the aggression between participants might turn against you, creating further potential for conflict.

Seeking compromise

The chair must balance conflicting demands, offer new ideas for compromise, and cajole participants into accepting outcomes less favourable than originally desired. A chairperson should be capable therefore of perceiving issues from various points of view and explaining the benefits of particular proposals. Equally, you may need to suggest caution and identify disadvantages to advocates of certain actions. Periodically, you should summarise the essential points of recent discussions and clarify the implecations of decisions reached.

Implementing decisions

Often, the chair assumes responsibility for ensuring that decisions taken within a meeting are actually carried out. Accordingly, you might have to write letters and memoranda to appropriate executives and monitor the progress of implementation of decisions.

Various styles of leadership are relevant for various situations. Problem solving meetings, for example, can be run in comparatively unstructured ways to encourage free interchange of ideas. Meetings where large amounts of information have to be transmitted, and where agendas contain very many items, need structured, relatively authoritarian procedures. Democratic leadership styles are appropriate for meetings where grievances are aired or where compromise outcomes are necessary. A relaxed style can sometimes defuse potential flashpoint situations.

Note that a chairperson can cause problems by dominating conversation, imposing arbitrary solutions or not giving meetings sufficient time to reach conclusions. Democratic chairing can lead to loss of effective control: sub-groups, each with a dominant participant, may arise to challenge your authority.

Skilful chairpeople promote discussion through putting carefully selected questions to the whole meeting or to individual members. Questions can be asked at the start of the meeting to stimulate participation or during the meeting to maintain its continuity. In consequence, the chair will draw out the knowledge, skills and experience of relevant parties assuming of course that participants are willing to express opinions on the questions asked; thus weaknesses in stated positions can be probed and all the implications of suggested actions examined. The problem, of course, is that replies to questions frequently raise yet more questions and the replies themselves might be phrased as questions. Confusion then ensues, issues are clouded and the participants have differing perceptions of the purpose of the debate.

Periodically, summarise what has been said and decided and make sure that everyone has been able to contribute, that all members are perfectly clear about what the decision means (particularly if it involves technical jargon) and what each person will have to do to achieve its implementation.

4

Time Management

Objectives

This chapter will help you to:

- identify ways in which you can improve the management of time of both yourself and others
- draw up personal timetables and plan your working day.

In management, time is a *resource* to be allocated optimally, just as any other. Time spent in a committee meeting, for example, could instead be devoted to a (possibly more productive) one-to-one counselling session with a colleague. The time used in writing a letter may be better used discussing an important order with a customer or perhaps in inspecting output on the factory floor. Choices are necessary: busy managers cannot do everything they would like, so *decisions* are required regarding the distribution of time among competing wants. Unfortunately, willing and enthusiastic managers experience time shortage problems more than others because their workloads constantly expand. Thus, when choosing which tasks to complete first, you must always take account of their opportunity costs — the cost of each activity in terms of alternatives foregone. You should rank activities in order of importance and consciously adjust the time devoted to each job — a few extra minutes spent reading a report might be worth two or three hours in a meeting.

Choosing priorities may not be easy, so you need to organise systematically your personal timetable with a view to maximising the *creative* output of each working day. Routine administration, tactical decision taking and day to day control involve duties that are scattered and prone to frequent interruption. Yet interruptions waste a great deal of time. Often, interruptions arise from unwanted communications — letters, telephone calls, memoranda etc — that disrupt more creative work. Thus, select some part of your working day (between two and three in the afternoon for instance, by which time all the day's mail will have arrived) for communications duties and stick to this rigidly. If a piece of routine correspondence cannot be completed by the end of this allotted period leave it until the following day when it will receive first priority. Where possible, handle each item of correspondence only once; much time is wasted through duplicated activity resulting from repeated consideration of the same item.

Economies of scale are available from grouping together similar tasks. Write all your letters and memoranda at the same time and make your telephone calls one after another. Plan your calls — have all the necessary information, files etc on your desk before picking up the receiver so that you will not have to ring again after looking up missing information. Jot down a list of all the points you wish to make during the conversation and write your notes on each call on separate pieces of paper. Most modern telephones have at least ten memories for commonly dialled numbers, so record these in a clearly visible position.

Activity

To get used to the idea of handling correspondence only once, spend a few weeks attaching a half sheet of paper to every letter, memorandum, report etc you receive on which you record every occasion you look at or otherwise deal with that item. You will soon discover how extensively you duplicate the attention you pay to particular correspondences and, importantly, which topics absorb most of your time.

If you deal with outside visitors, see them all during a prearranged period. Try to see people by appointment and keep discussions within appointed times. Casual callers should be discouraged (within reason — you do not wish to appear remote and inaccessible) or reserve a predetermined period for casual calls. Each category of task has its own 'set-up time' just like a production line — although in managerial work the 'tooling up' operation might be as much concerned with switching into an appropriate frame of mind as with technical considerations.

Overexertion, resulting perhaps in stress and other illnesses, can be caused by attempting to achieve creative goals while simultaneously trying to keep abreast of current communications and other routine duties. You need therefore to allocate your time systematically through setting goals, assigning priorities and identifying and eliminating time-wasting activities. Often, future workloads can be forecast, at least in outline. Prepare a schedule of anticipated activities built around the most critical of the future tasks and keep a diary to record how closely you adhere to the programme. Predict and list all jobs needing attention, attach priorities and estimate the time required for each activity. The actual times you spend on various tasks should then be monitored, recorded, and subsequently compared against the forecast schedule.

Plan your working day as you would plan a construction project. Pause at appropriate moments (say 10.30 am, 12.00 pm, 2.30 pm and 4.30 pm) to review your progress against predetermined intentions and make a note of the causes of delay. A useful (though drastic) remedial technique for the totally disorganised individual is to spend a couple of working days recording at precise 30-minute intervals exactly what he or she is doing, why, who with and how it fits in with his or her general work. Do this honestly for a few days and you will soon establish a picture of how effectively you manage your time.

Organisational techniques

Today, many technical devices are available to help you save time. The diary is the basic tool of time management,

Activity

To what extent do you plan your working day as outlined in the text?

While some of you may feel that the ideas put forward are too rigid, no planning at all will lead to chaos, inefficiency and stress. Those of you who simply react to events, should try some forward planning and prepare daily work schedules. Compare what you actually achieve with the goals set in the schedule.

In the next section you will be introduced to some of the modern electronic aids that will assist with the planning process.

representing at once a means for planning activities and a record of the time available for various tasks. Electronic diaries and other information technology based innovations greatly improve the manager's capacity to schedule activities efficiently.

Electronic diaries

An electronic diary, operated via a desktop computer (or a wordprocessor with a computing facility), records in its permanent memory all your appointments for as long ahead as you wish (several years if you so desire). You enter as much detail as you can about each appointment, so that recall of appointments on to a visual display screen can be presented under any one of several headings: name of appointee, date, time of day, nature of appointment etc. This enables you to analyse the *structure* of your activities, since you can ask the diary to list all your appointments relating to a particular type of work, category of appointee etc and thus identify the areas that absorb most of your time.

Electronic diaries may be 'networked' within a firm, between various subsidiaries of the same organisation or (increasingly) between different independent organisations. Networking means the linking together of computers and their peripherals (especially printers) so that information can be instantly transmitted from screen to screen, from printer to printer or from one person's screen to someone else's printer. Local networks are confined to a single organisation. Global networks, operated through telecommunication systems, may span the entire world.

Networked electronic diaries thus enable the appointments of several people to be synchronised simultaneously. Suppose you are a supervisor in a firm's accounts department and wish to arrange a meeting with three colleagues in the production, personnel and marketing departments of the same firm. You type an instruction to this effect into your own electronic diary which then activates the networked system into searching the electronic diaries of your three colleagues to establish a mutually convenient time for the meeting. Your colleagues are notified of your request for their presences at the meeting on the screens of their own VDUs when they next 'log in' to receive their electronic mail (see below).

Needless to say, networked electronic diary systems create special problems, such as:

- managers making appointments over the phone or in other conversations and forgetting to register them in their diaries
- failure to log-in to the system first thing every morning to determine the day's appointments
- not giving sufficient notice of days off or short holidays, and failing to report absences due to sickness.

If someone within the system puts you down for a meeting you do not wish to attend you must cancel the entry in your own diary, whereupon the cancellation is automatically transmitted to the diary of the initiator. Should you wish to attend but not on the day and time specified, you simply type in a message to this effect and the system searches not only your own diary but also those of other intended participants to find a new, mutually convenient, alternative date and time.

Electronic mail

Great improvements in personal organisation and efficiency are possible through the use of electronic communications with other people and organisations via desktop computers. To go

---

Self-check

The electronic diary appears to be a valuable aid, some even compiling work schedules and sounding alarm bells to remind you of an appointment. Identify the main reason why the system might fail.

Answer
The main problem is a human one, ie an individual must register appointments into the system in the first place and also the individual must log into the system each morning in order to find out the appointments for the day.

'on-line' you type an appropriate command on your terminal key board and your modem then automatically dials the number you want and connects you to the recipient's system. Thereafter, anything you type into your machine is sent down the telephone line to some other computer. In a commercial electronic mail (*Email*) system each user has a personal 'mailbox', which is a separate file on a computer disk 'dedicated' to that individual — a password and code number are needed for access to the file. Incoming messages are temporarily held in the mailbox until the recipient has accessed and read them, so that recipients need not be present when messages are transmitted. A complete set of messages may be sent at times previously specified by the sender (say, at 12.00 and 3.00 pm each day) and the same message can be sent simultaneously to several hundred users. When accessing your mailbox you choose either to 'scan' stored documents, in which case a list of headings of the documents appears on your VDU, or you read each item in full. Then you may delete messages, hold them for later action, copy them on to another disk or forward them (perhaps with added comments) to other users. The sender automatically receives an acknowledgement of safe receipt of the message.

Email is an excellent time saver and extremely cost effective. It removes the need to print hard copy messages prior to transmission and cuts the cost of postage, envelopes etc. Various companies provide Email services. Firms rent an account with the 'host' company and are allocated a block of account numbers which are then ascribed to named employees. Most systems operate at normal telephone charge rates, and it takes only a few minutes to send even long messages. Communication is instant (unlike the post or internal memoranda) and, in contrast to the telephone, the other person need not be there at the time of transmission. The problem is that you can only communicate with other people on the same commercial system.

If you spend much time away from your desk a cordless telephone may be useful. You might also consider obtaining a 'voice messager', which is a form of answering machine that not only enables callers to leave messages, but also allows callers to record and transmit an identical message simultaneously to anyone possessing a 'mailbox' within the system — a single call can be transmitted to several different people at the same time; recipients do not need to be in when the message is sent. Thus you avoid having to ring (or write to) several people with the same information and, of course, by *recording* your message for later transmission you escape being drawn into irrelevant conversations (however enjoyable) with the people you contact.

Keeping records

Records are necessary for three purposes: to store data for future reference, as a basis for rational decision taking and to maintain documentary evidence of communications. Keep records simple, easy to maintain and strictly relevant to your requirements. Prepare an inventory of all your information needs and list all the data you have to transmit to others. The inventory will probably include details of cost, output and other performance indices, staff records (appraisal reports, job histories, references, training programmes etc), health and safety records (including the dates of inspections of fire and other equipment), minutes of important meetings, plus copies of essential letters and memoranda. Records are used for planning and to enable you to justify past decisions. Often, records consist of forms or are compiled from data extracted from forms. If you have to design forms, make them simple, comprehensive and quick and easy to complete. The fewer the number of forms used in the department the better, so try to integrate forms or redraft them so they can be used for several tasks. Avoid the temptation to design special forms to gather information that is only infrequently needed — once a form is incorporated into the information gathering system it might stay there regardless of how often it is used.

Sometimes, all the forms within a department (indeed within an entire organisation) can be standardised, with common layouts and uniform dimensions to facilitate handling and storage. Instructions on how forms are to be filled in should be clear and precise. Forms should be big enough to contain all the information they are intended to gather and strong enough to withstand frequent transit and long retention periods. The data written down on a form should be easily read and extracted.

A form's structure should depend on the purpose for which it is intended. One regular complaint about form layout from those who must use forms is that insufficient space is provided for answers. Other complaints concern ambiguity about the data required, inadequate margins and insufficient delineation between sections. The best way to design a new form is to ask yourself a series of questions. Why is the form necessary in the first place, what objective does it seek to achieve and what would happen if the form was not produced? Who is to fill in the form (the answer to this question will determine its complexity and style of presentation) and under what conditions will the form be completed? A lengthy questionnaire for completion at home needs a different format from one that will be filled in hurriedly on the factory floor.

Periodically, all the forms currently in use should be assembled in order to eliminate any which have ceased to serve their original purpose. Some forms can be abolished entirely, others combined. The data being gathered might no longer be needed, or may be available elsewhere. The fewer forms there are the less has to be spent on paper, printing and filing cabinets. Too often, forms are distributed needlessly widely. Copies are sent to people and departments that have no interest in their contents. Apart from wastage of time and paper, excessive distribution can cause unanticipated stockouts of forms during periods of heavy demand.

Record keeping is boring and is thus frequently overlooked or delegated to subordinates, yet good records are essential for effective executive management. Have a clear out once every six months; out-of-date records are not worth maintaining. Note however that any document relating to a contract should be kept for at least six years (after which it ceases to be legally actionable) and anything to do with job evaluation or equal opportunities (job applications for example) for at least one year, after which time it is reasonable to suppose that no complaint will be registered (if it is it will not be considered by an industrial tribunal).

Self-check

When designing forms, identify four factors that should be considered.

Answer
— what objective does it seek to achieve?
— what would happen if it did not exist?
— who is to complete the form?
— under what conditions will it be completed?
— who has to use the information contained in the form?
— how, where and for how long will the form be kept?

The underlying objective of forms is to facilitate the gathering of information and standardise the method of presentation. Today, the information contained in forms will be fed into computers and this frequently dictates the layout.

Activity

Some people hate mornings and work best later in the day, while for others the reverse is true. It is common sense to complete the most demanding work tasks when you are most creative and able to cope with complex problems.

Take a quick look at yourself. During which part of the day are you at your best?

As you read on, you will see how this idea can be incorporated into structuring your working day.

Structuring the working day

You need to establish a schedule and follow it rigidly. Certain activities may be temporarily put off, others cannot be avoided — and might demand use of resources that have to be withdrawn from other activities. Since further urgent problems may follow immediately after the resolution of the one to hand there is a tendency for the busy manager to postpone indefinitely the proper consideration of less pressing matters. In consequence, a large backlog of petty administration accumulates and this, ultimately, itself becomes a major problem. You should avoid this situation arising by deliberately reserving some limited period each day exclusively for routine work. The best time for this is when you are tired, since then the relief of doing mundane duties helps you relax following the completion of more demanding activities.

If you are normally fresh and energetic during the first part of the morning, do your difficult work then — if conversely you are a person who 'warms up' as the day goes by, then do mundane work in the mornings and reserve the demanding tasks for later. A common mistake is to use intellectually productive hours for work that is interesting but which does not require the exercise of discretion or other intense mental effort. Suppose for example that you are most creative between 9.00 and 11.00 am. You open your mail at 9.15 am and immediately become immersed in petty administration. Your brain 'locks in' to the minor issues raised by the correspondence and you spend all morning dealing with these matters. By the time you come to consider more substantial problems you are too tired to attend to them properly so they are put aside and never fully resolved! The answer, in this case, is to have a strict rule *never* to deal with correspondence before (say) 4.00 pm. I suggest also that you read reports at the end of the day. Then you can plan your response to them for the following day and not become immediately immersed in unplanned activities resulting from their recommendations.

You must learn to deal with interruptions — to switch your attention from one thing to another and then back again — quickly and without loss of momentum to your work. Set aside some part of the day, even if only a half an hour, when you will not allow yourself to be interrupted for any reason whatsoever, and use this period for intellectually demanding tasks. The balance of your working day should be under *your* control and you should adjust the balance whenever the time spent on a particular activity becomes excessive.

Activity

If you find it difficult to get the right balance, consider initiating a personal 'time awareness' programme, beginning with an analysis of the distribution of your time among various classes of activity. Keep a diary and record everything you do. After a couple of weeks, extract a comprehensive list of all your duties. Alongside each item put a grade (A, B, C etc) to indicate its importance and state whether it was urgent or routine. Now rearrange the list in order of the priority of the tasks and ask yourself whether you devoted sufficient time to the top priorities. What proportion of your time do you estimate you spent on various categories of task? The answer may surprise you. Next, specify some proportion of your total time that you feel you *should* devote to each category and thereafter try to structure your day in these proportions.

Take care not to attend inessential meetings and leave a meeting early if the remaining items on the agenda do not concern you. Meetings can be enjoyable and by attending you remain 'in touch' with your colleagues, but they often waste time. The same applies to routine work which, although agreeable, could be done by someone else. You should not personally undertake too much simple work; equally, you ought not assume total responsibility for all difficult tasks — specialists can be consulted, committees established or outsiders engaged. Not only is difficult work potentially stressful, but it also takes longer to complete if a single person tries to do things that should be handled by a team.

A useful timesaver is to insist that all problems referred upwards by subordinates be accompanied by a recommended solution and that every report submitted begins with a summary.

Managing the time of others

Managers organise the time of their subordinates through delegating work to them, and through generally ensuring they are kept busy. Problems arise when subordinates lack effort and/or deliberately avoid work.

Work avoidance

Strategies for avoiding work fall into two categories: those which seek to minimise the intensity of effort expended in a job and/or which attempt to shorten the length of the working day (work 'reducing' strategies) and those which try to exchange easier or more enjoyable duties for work that actually needs to be done (work 'substitution' strategies). Work avoidance may be deliberate or unintended, although either variety is equally wasteful of time and annoying to other members of a working team. Premeditated strategems (such as persistent unpunctuality, taking unnecessary breaks, doing 'walkabouts' around the firm, appearing to be absorbed in a task while actually doing nothing, shifting files from one location to another, going somewhere half an hour before lunch and not returning until the lunchbreak has ended, etc) are well known and need little further discussion. These are 'knife-edging' strategies which balance the necessity of keeping a job against the overwhelming desire to avoid exertion. The employee does a modicum of work to avoid suspicion, but risks exposure and with it, the opprobrium of colleagues.

More interesting is the case where an individual evolves a refined and highly sophisticated set of task evasion strategies, yet is blissfully unaware of the fact. Your subordinate is not deliberately malingering (indeed, considerable effort might be required in implementing a strategy) but still achieves nothing! Here, instead of work *reduction* techniques being applied, collateral duties are invented to run in parallel with tasks that really need to be done, eventually crowding them out: the worker is (demonstrably) so busy performing contrived supplementary duties that he or she is unable to deal effectively with really important matters. Invariably the self-created tasks are easier and more interesting to perform than the employee's outstanding, and perhaps disagreeable, official workload. The extra tasks might be designed to enhance the job-holder's status and thus promote still further opportunities for involvement in irrelevant activities. Examples are the excessive amounts of time some people spend in meetings which have little significance for their work (but to which they want to be *seen* to contribute) and unnecessary involvement in interview panels for the selection of staff for other departments.

Further manifestations of the phenomenon include:

- time wasted on preparation for extraneous tasks, including the acquisition of additional knowledge, skills and experience needed to undertake them, plus higher expenditures on training as individuals create for themselves new areas of responsibility that require further skills and familiarisation
- detailed examination of colleagues' contributions to the supplementary activities, together with careful perusal of associated documents and correspondence, double-checking and complaining about minor errors (the time spent querying an insignificant mistake can exceed the time needed to perform a task)
- extra communication with higher management, especially requests for direction on unimportant matters
- employees finishing work before they should, because they are so exhausted by their marginally significant activities that they are too tired to complete the last hour or so of the working day.

What are the root causes of work avoiding behaviour and how does it relate to workers' perceptions of their employment role? Often, behaviour at work depends on desires for status, recognition of the value of contributions and on human needs for the establishment and maintenance of satisfactory personal relationships with others. In particular, the desire to be *seen* to be important can exert great influence — high status work is normally associated with taking decisions: it need not matter which particular decisions are taken, only that a certain individual be observed taking them. The problem, therefore, is to ascertain who should take various classes of decision and how delegation (see below) and decision taking procedures should be organised.

Your subordinates will probably have their own ideas about what constitutes a fair distribution of authority and responsibility within the department, and they may hold definite opinions regarding how much of their working day 'belongs' to the firm (quite independent of official working hours specified in contracts of employment) rather than being available for the pursuit of personal as distinct from organisationally imposed objectives. Ideally, formal divisions of working time and of authority and responsibility structures should correspond to divisions regarded as fair by your subordinates. In practice however, individual roles might be unclear: people may feel 'put on' by others, that they are being asked to do things beneath their dignity and/or which are not an integral part of their official duties. Petty resentments then arise. There are arguments about who should do what. Much energy is spent on uncoordinated activity.

Nothing gets done: individuals either assume that someone else will complete difficult or disagreeable tasks or they lack the resources or personal authority (perhaps even the inclination) to execute them. In consequence, real power becomes vested in unofficial leaders who possess the initiative and desire to seize it. Yet, the direction of leadership exercised by these individuals may not be that which senior management wishes to occur.

These are debilitating problems and there are no easy solutions. Note particularly the uselessness of conventional recipes for organisational efficiency within this context. Orthodox remedies such as greater precision in the drafting of job specifications, more detail in organisation charts, further specialisation, extensive supervision by senior management etc will not improve the situation. Indeed, the problem could well be made worse because such measures are bound to create numerous additional opportunities for work avoidance. Job descriptions and organisation charts, for example, become out of date so quickly in today's fast changing business conditions that rigid adherence to them generates great potential for legitimate non-performance of important duties. Cries of 'That's not my responsiblity, it's not in my job specification', or 'I can't do this without permission' resound through organisations attempting to tighten their job and responsibility description procedures.

The more precisely defined are the tasks which an employee *ought* to do, the greater the scope for declining to undertake work not strictly covered by a job description, and no organisation chart or job description can comprehensively define all possible tasks that an employee might reasonably be expected to perform. Ultimately, individuals must interpret their own roles and organisational status. Yet this very process of analysing and interpreting the wording of a job description, of expounding to others the organisational implications of the chain of command in a complicated line and staff system is itself time consuming and diverts attention from more pressing issues! Opportunities for obscurantist elaboration of individual roles and responsibilities abound. A devastating technique for work avoidance in such circumstances is for employees to remain silent about the fact that tasks allocated to them are beyond their job specifications and then use this fact, belatedly, as the justification for not having done the work.

There are perhaps five things you might do:

- allocate important and/or complicated duties to two (or even three) people to complete together. Each partner will complement and motivate the other and their joint experience can be brought to bear on a problem. Unconscious work avoidance is less likely when two individuals must jointly accomplish a task. Personal incompetence or malingering in one of the partners will soon be exposed and if partners are changed periodically then even if one or two colleagues of a malingerer have been persuaded to remain silent, the offending party must eventually be discovered

- introduce a system of task rotation so that different people are responsible for particular duties for set periods of (say) three, six or twelve months. Then, the success of the person currently responsible for those duties may be evaluated against successes achieved by predecessors in that same role

- issue to all members of your team a preprinted questionnaire asking them to specify what *they* feel they need from you in order to be able to work more productively. The form should begin with the words 'In order to do my job more effectively I need:', and then be followed by sections headed 'more of' and 'less of' in respect of various facilities and resources

- maintain an 'achievement register' listing all the major tasks that need to be done and the people responsible for them over the next month, quarter and perhaps even the next year. Update the achievement register periodically once a month and in so doing write out alongside each task that has *not* been completed a brief explanation of why this is so. Alongside each objective achieved, write the names of the people responsible for the result. A picture will then emerge of those key individuals who accomplish most things, which can be compared with the initial listing of the individuals who ought to have completed various tasks

- when dividing work into units for distribution to pairs of individuals or sections, allocate tasks to categories created around *types* of work rather than level of responsibility. Thus, someone who for example is good at negotiating can be given all work that embodies a major negotiating component. An expert communicator can be put in charge of all the external communications of the group, no matter how important or trivial. In consequence, all employees will have at least some higher status work to do and thus will *want* to structure their working time efficiently. Important tasks will be done first and workers will not finish their day's work before they should.

Delegation

Delegation is at once a technique for saving time and a management control method. It occurs within *all* organisations. In a limited company for example, the board of directors is elected by shareholders who delegate to the board the power to take strategic decisions; the board then delegates authority to senior managers in charge of functions or divisions, who then

Activity

Make a rough estimate of how much of your time is spent talking on the telephone, attending meetings, visiting other departments and speaking to colleagues. Have you got your priorities right? Could some jobs be cut out altogether? Are you doing jobs that could be given to someone else and, if so, which? Can you set aside certain parts of the day for important duties? Could you re-plan your day in order to avoid frequently changing from one type of task to another?

delegate to heads of department and so the process goes on. Delegation — the assignment of responsibilities to subordinates, accompanied by the devolution of authority necessary to implement decisions — is essential for efficient administration because managers do not have the time or specialist knowledge to take all important decisions. Care is necessary in the choice of duties for delegation, and managers must ensure that subordinates selected to receive delegated work are competent to complete it successfully. The recipients of delegated authority must be given all necessary resources, information and executive authority. Systematic delegation is crucial for management development programmes. Work of increasing difficulty can be delegated thus gradually improving a subordinate's capacity to act independently.

Self-check

What does the term 'delegation' mean to you?

Answer

Delegation is the assignment of responsibilities to subordinates, accompanied by the devolution of authority necessary to implement the decisions.

Excuses for *not* delegating abound: lack of confidence in subordinates' abilities, overestimation of your personal value, a feeling that you should be *seen* personally undertaking certain duties, fear that as they become increasingly competent your subordinates will eventually represent a threat to your job and so on. Yet failure to delegate is a prime reason for being constantly short of time (as well as demotivating subordinates through not involving them in higher level work) and you will, eventually, lose effective control of the situation simply through being inundated with work. You will become bogged down in detail, your staff will not initiate activity in your absence and will be unable to cope with crises when you are not there. Routine work will take a long time to complete, while major tasks will not be give proper attention. Ask yourself the following questions:

- can the task be delegated?
- should it be delegated?
- is there a person in the department capable of handling it?
- if not, should someone be trained?
- will a particular subordinate benefit from doing this work? How will the experience fit in with his or her career development?

You must decide what to delegate, when to delegate and in what circumstances. Delegate whenever your personal workload becomes excessive, when confronted by technical problems of a highly specialist nature or whenever you believe your subordinates will be better motivated, feel a greater sense of participation or will learn something useful from performing the tasks delegated. Be prepared to give up to subordinates some of the work you find particularly enjoyable — your staff will appreciate this and the loyalty it creates will more than pay you back in the longer term. For delegation to work, discernible chains of command are needed, so that everyone knows to whom they are responsible, the work they are expected to do and to what standards.

Review briefly the particular strengths and weaknesses of each of the people who work for you. List the skills and experience needed to perform each of the tasks you intend delegating and relate these to the attributes of various members of your team. Note importantly that it is not always appropriate to delegate a task to the *best* qualified subordinate, since you may wish to introduce a less experienced subordinate to new and different types of work.

What to delegate

Apart from saving your time, delegation can help you avoid stress, provided of course you do not need to worry about your subordinates' abilities to cope with the delegated work — and this itself will increase your efficiency. Work that has a high communications content (letter writing, first drafts of reports, telephone calls, routine meetings etc) might be your prime target for delegation, since you then avoid many of the frequent interruptions (ringing telephones, memoranda to be answered, dealing with suppliers and/or customers and so on) associated with routine communications. Bear in mind however that if you delegate too much repetitive administrative work to one person you could make his or her job intolerable. Try to plan your delegation as an integral part of a training and staff development scheme, not as a simple way of ridding yourself of distasteful duties.

Work that is particularly suitable for delegation includes fact-finding assignments, preparation of rough drafts for reports, investigation of feasibilities of possible solutions to problems or straightforward analysis of routine information. Make your subordinates' objectives clear and progressively increase the level of difficulty of the work delegated to them. Insist that subordinates present you with only brief, condensed accounts of their normal day-to-day activities but tell them always to come and see you whenever they find a recently delegated category of task too difficult to handle alone.

It is important to realise that some routine work is useful, in small measures, for relieving the stresses imposed by creative exertions. Heavy concentration that cannot be sustained for long periods is needed for important management work. Easier tasks, undertaken intermittently, can break up your day — your workload becomes more varied and your personal efficiency may increase. What point is there in delegating all your mundane duties if in consequence you spend long periods of complete inactivity when the inspiration for creativity has gone?

Several interpersonal relations difficulties can arise when delegating work, including the following.

- subordinates may come to perceive you as aloof and inaccessible, a figurehead who 'passes the buck' but who then declines to assume responsibility for the failure of projects which, from the outset, had no hope of success
- work could be delegated that is outside the normal and proper chain of command. An example is when a senior manager delegates to a supervisor responsibility for dismissing (say) casual or part time labour even though the senior manager (although he or she may not know this) has no legal authority to dismiss
- subordinates may feel you are disinterested in the work you delegate and, by implication, in them
- if subordinates do all the work but are not involved in taking final decisions based on their efforts their morale might fall, especially if they believe the final decisions are wrong
- frequent staff changes cause confusion over who is responsible for delegated work. A manager who leaves the firm may have delegated a task to a subordinate who might not inform the manager's incoming replacement that this is so. The work might then remain unfinished or not be satisfactorily completed. Always keep a record of the tasks you delegate.

Subordinates should never be made to feel that work is delegated to them only when you are confronted with difficult problems that you are not personally competent to handle, so always tell people *why* you want them to perform the delegated tasks.

Delegation is an excellent means for developing the talents of subordinates, especially in areas which require the exercise of discretion. However, subordinates will inevitably make mistakes as increasing amounts of authority and responsibility are delegated — many skills are learnt largely through experience and errors of judgement will certainly occur. These mistakes should be regarded as *normal* consequences of the delegation process. Always be ready to back up the decisions of your subordinates, even if you do not wholeheartedly agree with their actions.

Self-check

Identify two benefits and two problems associated with delegation.

Answer
Benefits are that it develops talents/skills of subordinates; frees managers from some routine tasks; motivates staff; aids management succession. Problems include lack of skill on part of subordinates; risk of mistakes; subordinates feel they do all the work without any of the glory; manager may delegate tasks he or she dislikes or deems unimportant.

Do not monitor your subordinates continuously as they complete delegated work. Constant checking stifles initiative and generates insecure feelings among junior staff. Delegation is difficult, moreover, where boss and subordinate do not share common perspectives about *how* problems should be solved. You ought not to specify in too much detail how you expect delegated work to be completed, since you need to develop your subordinates' independence and ability to assume personal responsibility for decisions, but take care to indicate the *form* of the problem solving activity you consider most appropriate for achieving the objectives you set.

5
Stress

Objectives

This chapter will help you to:

- develop ways of coping with stress in the work situation
- identify symptoms of stress both in yourself and others.

Management can be extremely stressful. Much managerial stress relates to conflicting and ultimately irreconcilable demands placed upon you by colleagues. Your team will expect you to support it in disputes with higher management while, simultaneously, superiors might insist that you represent senior management's views. Engineers may demand that your section's output be technically excellent, while at the same time the company accountant insists that you cut production costs. Similar conflicts can arise between demands for favourable treatment from competing subordinate groups. Resolution of such conflicts requires a high level of interpersonal skill and the problems involved can create stress.

Supervisory management, which is a link between higher management and the workforce, can be especially stressful. Supervisors control non-managerial employees, but are themselves directed by other managers who often are not personally involved with the workforce and thus might not understand the problems they face. And while supervisory managers perform all the *functions* of executive management (planning and organising work, command, control, coordination of effort etc), only rarely do they become involved in the *determination* of policy. To be good at supervision an individual needs to have a wide breadth of knowledge about organisation and management, practical communication, industrial relations, health and safety, indeed about all the topics covered in this book *plus* matters relating to quality control, production methods and the purely technical aspects of his or her firm and industry. In consequence, supervisors are regarded as all things to all people and this, in conjunction with their unique position midway between management and workers, can induce stress.

Activity

List those aspects of your job that you find stressful.

You should not feel embarrassed about experiencing stress in the workplace, as it need not reflect on your ability to do the job. While the actual aspects identified will vary, most will reflect conflicting demands made on an individual.

Remember also that stress possesses good and bad features, as you will see when you read on.

What is stress?

Stress has good and bad features. It provides the adrenalin needed to sustain intense effort and handle several complementary problems simultaneously. At the same time it drains your physical and emotional resources. You react to stress physiologically and psychologically. On encountering a dangerous situation you experience a release of hormones which drains blood from the skin and the digestive system, glucose and fat are released into the bloodstream and your breathing becomes more rapid. Continued exposure to a stressful environment causes tiredness, irritability, physical upsets such as headaches and rashes and possibly alterations in personality and behaviour such as excessive drinking or outward aggression. However, stress is not a *measurable* reality, its existence is apparent only through its consequences — how it *affects* individuals. Stress consists of an amalgamation of pressures and reactions and different people respond to stress in different ways. Most of us associate stress with the idea of pressure and of the consequences of reactions to pressure. Yet some managers thrive on pressure, it helps them draw on physical and emotional resources and they actually enjoy tense and challenging situations. Whether stress stimulates or debilitates depends largely on the background to the event and the duration of the experience. A short term skirmish is quite unlike a protracted war. Initial excitement can easily turn into long run distress.

Stress seems endemic to modern organisational life. Managers need therefore to understand its symptoms and causes and how to respond to its manifestations.

Activity

In the previous activity you were asked to look at yourself and now you must try to think in more general terms. As a manager, you must be alive to the causes of stress in others, ie subordinates and colleagues.

List as many causes of stress as you can in 5 minutes.

How many factors did you identify? Compare your list with that which follows.

At work, common causes of stress include the following:

- ambiguity over which tasks should take priority during the working day
- unclear self-identities, confusions over individual roles in management hierarchies
- perceptions by individuals that they are not competent at their jobs
- frustration and the feeling that promotion opportunities have been unfairly blocked
- feelings of personal inadequacy and insecurity
- conflicting demands put on people by superiors who impose different, incompatible objectives

- lack of communications with superiors and colleagues
- bad personal relationships with fellow employees, customers, suppliers or other contacts outside the organisation.

Often, stress results from overwork. The overload may be quantitative (having too much work to do) or qualitative (finding work too difficult). Long working hours often involve a poor diet, lack of proper exercise, inadequate relaxation and deteriorating interpersonal relationships. People whose knowledge, skills, aptitudes and experience are insufficient for satisfactory performance in their jobs are rarely willing to admit that this is so, fearing loss of status and respect from colleagues, perhaps even demotion. Otherwise, the range of things that could cause stress is seemingly endless. Deadlines, anxieties about the slow progress of a project, lack of control over situations, inadequate resources, petty rules and restrictions, aggressive colleagues etc.

Symptoms of stress

Since there are so many potential causes of stress it is better to focus attention on identifying its symptoms. The existence of stress becomes manifest in how a person functions (physically and psychologically) and behaves.

Physical manifestations

Stress related illnesses may result directly or indirectly from stress inducing activities. Coronaries, for example, can result from stress created restlessness, hyper-activity, impatience and general angst. Equally, illnesses might be caused by excessive smoking, drinking, inadequate diet, lack of sleep etc resulting from stress. Less dramatic physical manifestations of stress include high blood pressure, excessive cholesterol levels, abnormal cardiogram readings, weight loss and skin complaints. Moreover, fainting, frequent profuse sweating and severe headaches regularly afflict those who suffer from prolonged and severe stress. Exhaustion, depression and feelings of alienation from the working environment are also common. Many of these physical manifestations are psychosomatic in origin. Among the most frequent psychosomatic illnesses (ie those which emanate from emotional tension) are indigestion, cramp, backache and insomnia.

Psychological effects

Anxiety is perhaps the clearest indicator that someone is unable to cope. It affects abilities to concentrate and relax, creates irritability and generates feelings of malaise and unease. Perceptions are affected — stress ridden individuals may become irrational, emotionally volatile and excessively suspicious. Psychological and physical factors do of course interact — stress related worries have unpleasant side effects on physical health. Perhaps the most immediate consequence of prolonged exposure to stress is a constant feeling of tiredness due to the combination of the draining effects of emotional conflict, overwork, lack of sleep and general anxiety. Employees who experience stress created fatigue will be dull, clumsy, unable to think clearly or perform work for long periods.

Changes in behaviour

Work performance typically deteriorates when individuals experience protracted exposure to high levels of stress. The direction of a person's response is difficult to predict. Some individuals become antagonistic, others withdraw into themselves. Tension, tiredness and anxiety often lead to outbursts of hostility and aggression. Workers become oversensitive to criticism and increasingly unable to relate to friends and working colleagues. Sleep patterns alter, daytime tiredness ensues. The general rundown in a person's health can lead to frequent colds, upset stomachs and other minor illnesses. Routine errors become more frequent. Stress prone individuals have more accidents than others. Many people respond by taking tranquillisers (or conversely anti-depressants), smoking heavily (with consequent health problems) or by drinking excessive amounts of alcohol. Marital and other family difficulties are common among stress ridden people.

Stress, then, imposes significant costs on the individual. Yet no manager can entirely avoid stress. You must, therefore, learn how to *manage* stress, to modify your perceptions and behaviour in response to stressful events; otherwise, if you soldier on as if stress were not present, your health and personal efficiency may be greatly impaired.

Self-check

The text mentions three categories of symptoms of stress: physical manifestations, psychological effects and changes in behaviour. Give three examples of each.

Answer

Physical manifestations: coronaries; excessive smoking and drinking; high blood pressure; weight loss; rashes; headaches; exhaustion; depression; indigestion; fainting; sweating.

Psychological effects: anxiety; fatigue; clumsiness; inability to concentrate; irrational behaviour; suspicion.

Changes in behaviour: deterioration of standard of work, withdrawn, oversensitive to criticism, aggressive, prone to frequent illnesses, accident prone, use of pills and/or alcohol.

You must remember that the factors mentioned can be symptoms of problems other than stress. However, anyone displaying any of the symptoms should give you cause for concern and indicate that some further investigation is needed.

Coping with stress

First, recognise and accept that stress is an inevitable feature of your job. Do not try to repress feelings of anxiety. If you deny their existence you create for yourself a fantasy situation almost guaranteed to promote eventual worry and distress. In particular, do not assume that other people will do anything to help you overcome stress — they have enough to do looking after their own apprehensions. Rather, expect the worse — assume that symptoms of your stress will be misinterpreted in the most unsympathetic and unfavourable possible ways. Take full responsibility for your thoughts and actions.

Neurotic anxiety often causes the victim to 'sublimate' a problem. All the person's nervous energies are directed towards attainment of an *irrelevant* objective, unrelated to the source of the stress. For example, a supervisor whose production figures are hopelessly inadequate might devote lavish attention to personnel and welfare matters, replacing the need to tackle fundamental production difficulties with unnecessary concern for trivial issues. Be aware of this possibility, and recognise also that when under severe stress you might wrongfully attribute to others responsibility for your neurotic state. Once you acknowledge the existence of these dangers you have overcome the first hurdle in coping with stress related aspects of supervisory work.

Delegation is the obvious way to overcome work overload, provided of course the subordinates to whom work is delegated are capable of successfully completing the delegated tasks. The problem here is that if you do not have complete confidence in your subordinates' abilities you will worry about the work not being done, resulting in even greater amounts of stress. A useful strategy is that of predetermined withdrawal from particularly stressful activities. Thus, whenever you feel that things are really getting on top of you, make out a list of stressful events with which you will refuse to become involved. For instance, you might decide in advance to abandon a forthcoming committee meeting if certain occurrences or people are discussed. Likewise, you might predetermine a personal workload beyond which you will decline to undertake additional duties.

An idea I personally find *extremely* useful, though it may at first sound bizarre, is to reserve (say) 30 or 40 minutes towards the end of the working day *just* for worrying about work and nothing else (though only rarely do I worry for anything approaching this period — ten minutes is the norm). If my mind begins to wander towards stress inducing subjects before my prearranged worry period I consciously defer consideration of them until the allotted time. I simply jot down a note of the issue to remind me to worry about it later. Another idea is to maintain a 'stress diary' in which you record all incidents that cause you stress. This, of course, is only worthwhile if you suffer significantly; otherwise you will never get around to filling it in (which fact indicates that you are not experiencing undue stress). After you have completed such a diary for a few weeks a distinct pattern of events (and people) that cause you extreme stress will emerge. Then you can take appropriate action, either by consciously avoiding these events and/or individuals or, if this is not possible, by at least anticipating that involvement with them will be stressful, so that you are prepared for and thus better able to respond to the likely stress. The diary is entirely confidential, so there is no reason why you should not write a list of the particular people and situations most likely to cause you distress. Describe them literally and comprehensively.

Relaxation

While useful, 'anticipatory coping' is not always feasible in practice since you may not be able to predict when stressful incidents are likely to occur and even if you do identify the source of potential trouble you still need the ability to accommodate the problem. Two things can help: the capacity to relax and the use of personal assertion.

In seeking to relax you seek to harmonise your body and mind in an acceptable, predetermined rhythm. Stress generates high levels of adrenalin, which upset the physical system by preparing it for violent action which does not actually occur. Hard physical exercise — running, aerobics, a workout in a gym — will work off excess adrenalin, as indeed will an explosive loss of temper (which is why people often feel relaxed following an angry outburst). Unfortunately, few employing organisations currently possess workout facilities (though some progressive firms have in fact installed small multi-gyms for the use of executive employees) and since angry behaviour at work is not socially permissible it is usually necessary to try to relax in alternative, non-physically exertive ways.

To relax, you must increase your intake of oxygen in order to burn off surplus energy. Withdraw for a few minutes from the stressful environment, preferably to somewhere you will be alone. Sit down, keeping your back perfectly straight and your legs together. Focus your mind on a point in the centre of the lower region of your stomach. Half close your eyes and inhale quietly and deeply for approximately seven seconds. Hold and let the air circulate for a further three seconds, then exhale slowly. Repeat the cycle several times, breathing through your stomach rather than through your chest and remembering always to keep your back straight. While doing this, wipe out *all* thoughts from your mind — concentrate on thinking about nothing. By controlling your thoughts and breathing in this way, even for just a few minutes, you cultivate the mental composure and stability necessary to return to the stressful situation you left earlier. Then, while you are actually in the stressful environment, try tensing groups of muscles, starting with the neck and shoulders and working downwards, for a few seconds and then deliberately relaxing them. By the time you reach your toes your mental state should have considerably improved.

Activity

Try this method of relaxation the next time you are in a particularly stressful situation. Obviously, you may be unable to rush out of a meeting but try to find a few moments as soon as possible after it has ended.

Although a loss of temper might help *you* to relax, avoid such outbursts because they adversely affect other people. In overcoming your own stress, you *create* stress for others and there is a natural tendency to vent anger on innocent subordinates who cannot easily answer back rather than on the colleagues responsible for the stressful problem. It is unfair to expect other people to have to accommodate your anger. Assertiveness, on the other hand, can be most helpful in dealing efficiently with stressful situations. Assertion (see Chapter 2) is quite different from aggression in that when acting assertively you seek to be clear, direct, open and honest rather than to bully or coerce. Once you convince yourself of your fundamental *right* to be doing your work in your chosen manner and of your *right* to make the occasional mistake and try again, then your job will become less stressful. Thus, you will not worry if projects sometimes go awry. If you are asked to take on too much work you will be able to say no without feeling guilty and if you do not understand something you will ask, without embarrassment, for clarification. You will not constantly feel the need to justify yourself. If you are not given enough time, resources or authority to complete allotted tasks you will inform your superiors, firmly and without hesitation.

Organisational factors

Firms and other employing organisations can attempt to minimise the stress experienced by employees. Counselling services can be established; performance appraisals and other staff development activities can be designed to incorporate mechanisms for identifying workers likely to suffer from stress. The division of labour might be consciously applied to stress inducing activities in order to spread the load of this type of work. Sometimes, jobs can be restructured to remove stressful elements. Then, the stressful aspects of several jobs can be combined into a new job undertaken by someone *specially trained* and experienced in coping with stress. Training, generally, is good for reducing feelings of stress in employees; for three reasons:

- the worker's sense of occupational competence increases following the acquisition of new skills
- feelings of personal esteem are enhanced (the employee is treated as an important person for the duration of the course)
- training temporarily separates individuals from their normal working enviroments, enabling them to reflect on the nature of their jobs, compare their experiences with

those of fellow trainees, and see their work in its proper perspective.

Depression

Depression is an especially damaging possible consequence of stress induced chronic fatigue and anxiety. The term 'depression' means permanent feelings of dejection and apathy, which can be caused by things other than stress. The cause of a work related depression may be either *exogenous*, such as failure to achieve an important objective or disappointment at (say) not gaining promotion, or *endogenous* (within the person) resulting perhaps from innate feelings of hopelessness, personal inadequacy and inability to cope. Depression manifests itself in abnormal sleep patterns, listlessness, lethargy and agitated behaviour. Loss of appetite and libido may also occur. Depressed people tend to avoid contact with others and not interact in socially conventional ways.

In work contexts, depressions are worsened if employees perceive that they have no control over depressing situations. Participation in decision making, provision of training and staff development opportunities, job rotation and involvement of individuals with teams (rather than working in isolation) may therefore alleviate some depressing circumstances. Long working hours can cause depression. They restrict social interaction outside work and leave little time for leisure, or indeed for simple rest and recuperation.

People react to unpleasant events in different ways. Thus, being passed over for promotion may cause one person to become angry, another to become depressed, a third to breathe a sigh of relief at not having to assume extra responsibility. If this incident is followed by a belief that promotion will *never* come then the affected individual might experience despair, whereas belief that the decision was fundamentally unfair could lead to an outburst of anger. Hence, whether an event causes depression depends crucially on how it is perceived and you may be able to assist colleagues in this respect by helping them to clarify issues and see them in a proper perspective — a reinterpretation of a depressing incident might transform its psychological consequences.

Helping a depressed colleague

Severe mental depression is, of course, a serious illness requiring specialist medical treatment, possibly involving the use of drugs. However, convincing someone to seek proper medical advice can be difficult. If you have a colleague who is acutely depressed try pointing out that depression is today recognised as a legitimate medical illness and that it *can* be cured. Many severely depressed people are perplexed and confused by their emotions; they feel physically ill, but are reluctant to seek proper medical advice because of the absence of *physical* signs of illness — there is no rash, bruise, cut or other dramatic visible manifestation to show the doctor! Depressed people do not understand themselves and typically do not expect others to understand them either.

Emphasize that your colleague can almost certainly look forward to a recovery. Comment that *everyone* becomes depressed occasionally, and that given what has happened to your colleague he or she *has every right* to feel miserable. If the depression is situational and not especially distressing, you may well be able to talk your colleague through the experience. Reassure the person that his or her reaction is reasonable, that he or she is not behaving irresponsibly or without good cause — look for rational justifications for your colleague feeling depressed. For serious endogenous depressions, do actively encourage your colleague to see a doctor. Say this directly — your advice will probably be welcome because seriously depressed people do not enjoy being depressed and will gladly accept the possibility of alleviation.

Depression is a wretched experience and those who have been severely depressed greatly fear its recurrence. Paradoxically, therefore, the dread of becoming depressed in future can itself cause feelings akin to depression. As a supervisor, you can definitely help in this respect. Apart from offering support and general counselling, suggest to your colleague that he or she keep a 'depression inventory' recording all the things that cause feelings of depression, assigning a score to each incident on a scale of (say) one to ten. The causes of your colleague's depression might then be more accurately identified and potentially depressing situations consciously avoided. Inventory items can be expanded at length, with categories for particular personal relationships, avoidable and non-avoidable depressing events, items causing frustration, items causing feelings of personal inadequacy and so on. Simple as it is, this approach can be extremely helpful, since one of the first casualties of depression is a breakdown in the individual's ability to rationalise the causes of distress.

Often, an outsider can recognise links between particular events and changes in a person's behaviour that the affected individual does not notice. Depression, even today, is not a *socially* acceptable illness and sufferers are often deeply ashamed that it happened to them. It is easy, therefore, for a depressed person (wrongly) to feel isolated, misunderstood and entirely alone. Just by listening, by offering support and companionship during moments of crisis, you can play an important and valuable role in assisting that person objectively reappraise his or her situation, dispassionately and without attributing blame.

6

Managing a Team

Objectives

At the end of this chapter you will be able to:

- define what is meant by a group and a team
- recognise the importance to individuals of belonging to a group
- distinguish between formal and informal groups
- operate as an effective team leader
- handle conflict situations.

Work is a social activity; few people work entirely alone. Groups emerge within work organisations through the specialisation of functions, through the creation of teams to handle projects or naturally in order to satisfy a social need. Groups may be formally established by management or they might arise informally and spontaneously among the workers. Formal groups are set up to perform specific tasks: decision taking, project completion, problem solving, communication and so on. The key issue with formal groups is how best to direct, control and coordinate their activities. Should management impose highly structured group processes, with explicit and rigid roles and conventions or should the group itself be made responsible for its internal organisation? Informal groups result simply from people intermingling in working situations. Workers establish customs and social relations among themselves; patterns of behaviour are constituted, informal rules, relations and working methods not shown in organisation charts or official staff manuals become entrenched.

Activity

You are aware of the difference between formal and informal groups. Consider your own department for a moment. How many formal groups can you identify? Are there any informal groups? If so, do the informal groups conflict in any way with work of the department?

We will return to the difficulties that arise when informal groups seem to work against the formal groups later in the chapter.

Roles

The concept of 'role' is crucially important for a person's self-perception of his or her occupational status and of the value of a job in comparison with those of others. Role theory concerns how individuals behave, how they feel they *ought* to behave and how they believe other people should respond to their actions. A role is a total and self-contained pattern of behaviour typical of a person who occupies a social position. Accordingly, people occupy many roles during the course of their lives — as husbands or wives, mother or father figures, as 'office boys' (or girls), supervisors, senior managers etc. Individual interpretations of roles within a group define the pattern of group interrelations, perhaps even the group's entire structure and organisation.

Associated with each role is a set of standards and norms of conduct that the role occupant (and others) expect from holders of the position. A supervisor, for example, might be expected to behave, perhaps even to dress and speak, in a certain manner. The term *role category* describes a complete class of persons occupying a particular social position ('leader', 'old person', 'mother', 'senior executive', etc). Role expectations are then attached to the role category. A role expectation differs from a social norm in that whereas a norm (ie a behavioural expectation common to all group members against which the appropriateness of individual feelings, conduct and performance may be assessed) applies to *everyone* in a group, a role expectation is specific to the individual.

People expect they will behave in a certain manner in a particular situation, and typically possess definite expectations concerning the conduct of others. Such expectations are important because they guide individual actions. For example, colleagues who have worked together for several years usually possess efficient, smoothly functioning relationships because they know exactly how their workmates are likely to behave — each person anticipates the other's reactions to various situations and then adapts his or her own behaviour in appropriate ways.

A self-perceived employment role might involve a certain appearance (for example, senior managers may want to dress differently to their subordinates, to 'look the part'), or a particular manner or means of expression (accent, intonation, style of language, etc) may be required. Manifestations of a role (such as a certain mode of dress) provide information to others about how they should act towards the role occupant. Such external signals provoke definite attitudes concerning how others inwardly feel they ought to behave in interactions with that person.

Through experience, individuals eventually form role categories into which people of the various occupational classes they encounter may be placed. A supervisor, for instance, may be expected to behave in an authoritarian manner, regardless of that person's personality, background or general approach to management affairs. These categorisations simplify social interrelationships, since it is not then necessary to analyse every situation the individual meets. Rather, the person merely assumes a certain mode of behaviour in the other party, using this preassumption to guide his or her her reactions to events.

Groups

Whereas formal groups are deliberately constituted by management, informal groups develop without assistance or support. In a formal group, management selects members, leaders and methods of doing work. The group may be defined with respect to a task, function, status within the managerial hierarchy (such as members of the Board of Directors) or length of service with the firm (long serving employees might receive privileges not available to others and hence constitute an identifiable group). Formal groups are characterised by a high degree of managerial involvement in coordinating, controlling, and defining the nature of the activities they undertake.

Informal groups can form without management support. They are established by people who feel they possess a common interest. Members organise themselves and develop a sense of affinity to each other and a common cause. Often, it is an informal group that actually determines working methods and the quantity of work done. Hopefully, the aims of the informal groups that spring up within an organisation will correspond to the organisation's objectives, but they might not. Indeed, informal groups could form to oppose the wishes of management. A sensible management will thus recognise the importance of informal groups for organisational efficiency or their potential for disrupting organisational plans.

A further important distinction is between primary groups and secondary groups. A primary group consists of members who come into direct face to face contact with each other. Secondary groups are larger, less personal and lack immediate direct contact between members. Examples of primary groups are small departments within a firm, project teams, families, sports teams or other direct contact recreational associations. Membership of such a group often provides social and psychological support during times of stress. Secondary groups might be factories, communities, long assembly lines where workers do not come into contact with each other or geographical divisions of a company. These groups will be less solid and cohesive than primary groups, though interactions between members will still occur. Within primary groups, communications are rapid and direct.

Self-check

Why is it important for management to recognise the influence that informal groups can exercise?

Answer
Unlike formal groups, informal groups are formed voluntarily, often because the members share a common interest. They have the potential to act for or against the objectives of the organisation and management ignores such groups at their peril.

As you read on you will see the extent to which informal groups can influence standards of behaviour, working methods, output etc.

Group norms

Membership of a group helps a person interpret everyday events, identify his or her role in an organisation and satisfy social needs for involvement with others. The group supports and reinforces the individual's view of the outside world and this greatly encourages conformity to 'group norms'. A group norm is a shared perception of how things should be done or a common attitude, feeling or belief. Norms will exist about working methods, about how much work should be done (and how enthusiastically), about the quality of output, relations with management (and trade unions), how various people should be addressed and treated etc. Norms are particularly important in determining workers' attitudes towards change, since norms can create or overcome resistance to new ideas and working methods.

As norms emerge, individuals start to behave according to how they feel other group members expect them to behave. Initially, entrants to an existing group feel isolated and insecure and hence will actively seek out established norms to guide them on how they ought to behave. Norms facilitate the integration of an individual within the group and thus will be eagerly accepted by new members. They are soon internalised into entrants' personal value systems and help bind individuals to groups. In consequence, groups are often resistant to change. Members become set in their ways and attitudes and come to believe that the group norm is always correct, no matter what the circumstances. Any deviation from a norm has to be explained and justified by the individual to other members and if the deviation is not accepted by the group the deviant member is socially isolated.

Membership of a group provides individuals with companionship, social experience, opportunities for self-expression and social intercourse. Against these benefits, however, individuals must be prepared to modify their behaviour to fit in with group norms. The greater the value the individual places on group membership the more he or she will want to conform. Feelings of attachment increase and the power of the group to compel obedience to established norms is enhanced. Eventually, group behaviour settles down to a fixed routine. New entrants are expected to conform and to demonstrate their willingness to abide by group norms. The group can then continue to function despite changes of personnel.

Conflicts and contradictions within the group now begin to emerge, caused (for example) by:

- new technology which demands new working methods and/or new divisions of labour among group members
- members perceiving group objectives differently
- breakdowns in communications between group members
- personal disputes
- changing expectations of what might reasonably be demanded from membership of the group.

Such conflicts create the need for readjustments in internal group relations, including perhaps the introduction of new group norms.

Group cohesion

Group cohesiveness is the degree to which members are prepared to cooperate, content to work together and share common goals. High cohesion results in high productivity and morale. A cohesive group will support, in thought and action, the continuing existence of the group and its present activities. Cohesion encourages conformity to group norms and causes stable behaviour within groups, but the increased pressures for conformity can stifle initiative. Several factors contribute to the creation of group cohesion, including how often its members come into contact with each other, members' enthusiam for group objectives and the exclusivity and/or homogeneity of members of the group. The more frequently and intimately the members interact the more they will perceive themselves as a distinct group. If membership is selective, members feel a sense of achievement in being admitted and to the extent that members share a common background, education, age, outlook, ethnic or social origin etc they will be like-minded and share common perspectives.

External environments can also affect group cohesion. An environment consists of a multitude of physical, technological and social circumstances. If individuals see their environment as hostile they will feel great affinity to any group offering protection from external threat. Other factors conducive to cohesion are as follows:

- how easily members can communicate within the group. Poor interpersonal communications will inhibit the emergence of a collective sense of purpose. Note that a group is more likely to be internally cohesive the less contact it has with other groups
- the nature of the task to be completed. Individuals engaged on identical or very similar work are more likely to see themselves as a group than others. Incentive schemes can encourage cohesion; a group that is able to reward or punish its own members can exert great pressure on individuals to conform.

Self-check

What benefits does group cohesion bring?

Answer
— High staff morale and willingness to work together towards common goals
— Recognised and stable standards of work and behaviour
— Loyalty to the group and supportive atmosphere.

Cohesion is a most attractive feature in a working group, causing high morale, strong interpersonal relations and reinforcement of individual perceptions. The activities of a cohesive group are easy to coordinate since the group itself will monitor the efficiency of its operations. Members are encouraged to work hard in support of the group and may derive great satisfaction, even excitement, in so doing. Unfortunately, such enthusiasm might be directed against management, since powerful informal groups can arise to oppose management's wishes. Moreover, high group cohesion need not be associated with high productivity, low absenteeism and labour turnover, enthusiasm for work and other desirable characteristics, but rather the reverse. Cohesive groups might conspire to restrict output, perhaps even to disrupt the organisation's work.

Power and authority

Formal groups have appointed leaders. Informal groups have leaders who emerge naturally from the ranks of the group. Within a formal group, an unofficial leader might arise and function in parallel with the appointed leader. Unofficial leaders are important and their influence is sometimes formally recognised (for instance through the unofficial leader becoming a departmental shop steward). They exercise authority, albeit intermittently, but have no formal power as such. Formal leaders offer stability (appointed leaders are permanent, they remain despite changes in the structure of the group) and a focus for group identity. Usually, they can impose formal rules on individual members. Supervisors, for example, might be empowered to select individuals for better paid tasks, to recommend workers for promotion and might be authorised to suspend or dismiss subordinates. Often, leaders are appointed on the basis of their expertise in a function corresponding to that for which the group was formed. A typing pool supervisor, for example, is often a highly skilled and experienced typist. The chairperson of a problem solving committee typically has particular ability in the technical aspects of the problem area. Official leaders are responsible for communicating with other groups and for expressing the collective opinions of the group. In practice, however, unofficial leaders are frequently the people who actually direct and motivate others.

There are important differences between authority, influence and effective power. Influence is the effect of one person on the behaviour of others. It may be exercised by either formal or informal leaders and can operate through suggestion, persuasion, example or threat of sanctions. Authority is the *right* to control. In a supervisory context this might involve the determination of subordinates' workloads, taking decisions on behalf of the group, giving orders, possibly recommending pay rises or initiating disciplinary action. Formal authority is often accompanied by outward displays of status: different clothing (such as managers wearing suits while operatives wear overalls), separate canteens, different modes of speech and behaviour. These may even differ for each of several levels of authority within the managerial hierarchy. Lower ranks are expected to treat superiors with deference and respect. There is a clear system of command, coordination and control.

Power, in contrast, is a quality that other people *perceive* an individual to possess, giving that person the ability to influence the actions of others. An employee might have low occupational status and occupy no formal leadership role yet still exert enormous power within the organisation. Appointed leaders may or may not be powerful, depending on the following factors:

- their ability to coerce others into obedience through threats of punitive action
- personal charisma
- group members' willingness to accept the directions of appointed leaders
- the extent to which group members identify with the values of appointed leaders
- appointed leaders' abilities to satisfy group members' needs
- whether group members perceive appointed leaders to possess expert knowledge about the activities on which groups are engaged
- the extent to which members feel that a formal leadership

position is legitimate, say because of seniority within the group

- control over information, resources and access to higher levels of formal authority.

Group members who possess much power but little formal authority are fortunate in that they do not have to take the blame when things go wrong. Appointed leaders, however, have to accept the consequences of their actions. If they make bad decisions they are expected to pay. In consequence, official group leaders are often reluctant to take crucial decisions, either passing difficult problems upwards to higher management or ignoring them in the hope that other group members (those with power) will quietly sort them out. Responsibility, then, is a constraint on the exercise of authority, and might restrain the exercise of power.

Self-check

Distinguish between power, authority and influence.

Answer

Authority is the right to control and make decisions. It is vested in an individual by a higher authority and is associated with the position held.

Influence is the ability of an individual to affect the behaviour of others and may stem from one's formal status or from one's personality.

Power is a quality that other people perceive an individual to possess. It may stem from one's personality or from one's position within the organisation.

Organisational culture

How groups form — their norms, working practices and patterns of interaction — depends in part on the culture of the organisation (sometimes referred to as *organisational climate*) consisting of its customary ways of doing things and its members' shared perceptions of issues affecting the organisation. A firm's culture evolves gradually, and employees may not even be aware that it exists. Organisational culture is important, however, because it helps define how workers feel about their jobs. A culture will have arisen within a specific environmental context and be related to particular organisational needs. The problem is that an organisation's needs and activities alter, while its underlying culture remains. Culture involves common assumptions about how work should be performed and about appropriate objectives for the organisation, for departments within it and for individual employees.

Common perspectives

In a well managed firm, employees at all levels of authority will share common perspectives about the factors that determine its prosperity and future prospects. Such perspectives concern the guiding principles that govern the firm's work; how things should be done, when, by whom, and how enthusiastically.

To some extent these perceptions may be created by management *via* its internal communications, style of leadership, organisation system and working methods; but they can only be sustained and brought to bear on day-to-day operations by the firm's workers. Staff should *feel* they possess a common objective. They need to experience a sense of affinity with the organisation and to *want* to pursue a common cause.

The existence of common perspectives helps employees interpret day-to-day events and to structure and reinforce their views about the company.

Activity

Prepare a list of ten words or phrases which in your view . . . accurately sum up the culture of your employing organisation. The list might include such words as paternalistic, progressive, easy-going, autocratic, etc. Now ask a couple of people who work for you to do the same. Compare your list with theirs and identify differences. What do the differences tell you about attitudes within the department?

Group structures

Well-constructed groups can greatly enhance employee commitment, job satisfaction and sense of purpose. Specialised skills develop within groups; members collaborate, liaise, offer help and advice to others and generally interact through their work. Note, however, that working in groups is not always more efficient than working alone. Frequent disturbances from colleagues and the need to consult before taking action can retard progress and constantly irritate the individual worker. You need therefore to seek ways of making group work enjoyable and able to fulfil individual members' social needs. In particular, you must prevent informal groups from taking over the functions that official (management created) groups should undertake.

When creating groups (eg through establishing project teams to achieve particular objectives) try to keep group sizes reasonably small. Groups of more than a dozen people require extensive supervision and internal communications become difficult. Much time is spent coordinating group activities and decision taking is slow. Large groups encourage the emergence of sub-groups and factions differentiated in terms of status, length of service, opinions on social and work issues etc.

Encourage joint decision-taking within groups. Participation improves morale and stimulates cooperation; it facilitates the flow of information through the group and the emergence of new ideas. Reassure group members that their contributions will be taken seriously and that they are free to express opinions. Of course, complex problems require careful and detailed analysis and not all the group members will be capable of understanding the issues involved. In this case you (or the group leader to whom you have delegated official command of a subunit) should inform all the group members of the nature of the difficulties and how those members selected to handle these complex problems intend tackling them.

Define group objectives clearly and precisely. Members should see the point of what they are doing and how it fits in with wider organisational goals. Sound leadership is essential. As an appointed group leader you have to motivate, direct, set standards and monitor subordinates' performances. You allocate work to members, clarify issues and explain what needs to be done, settle disputes among members, resolve grievances and generally keep the peace.

A particularly important leadership role is that of introducing new members to the norms of the group. Newcomers, initially, feel anxious about their status and look to whoever they perceive as the group leader for clues regarding how they should behave. At first, formal rules will be followed to the letter, even if personal identities are sacrificed in the process. Then, as newcomers are gradually absorbed into the group, they learn to manipulate its conventions. They come to terms with other members and begin to assert their independence.

Groups function more efficiently if their leadership can be easily transferred. Critical dependence on a single person leads to the total collapse of the group when its leader resigns. Ensure, therefore, that someone is trained and ready to take over your group should you be transferred, promoted, temporarily absent or leave the firm.

Self-check

List the duties performed by a group leader.

Answer
Duties are likely to include allocation of work, motivation, monitoring results, settling disputes and grievances. The group should look to its leader for guidance, but should not be so dependent on the individual that it will cease to function, should the leader be absent for any reason.

Working groups can adopt one of three organisational structures: the hierarchy, the network, or the team. Hierarchies typically exhibit a pyramid form of authority and decision-making, with a distinct chain of command from the apex of the organisation to its base. There is a single group leader whose immediate subordinates themselves possess immediate subordinates through clearly defined spans of control. Each person is accountable only to his or her immediate superior in the hierarchy.

A *network*, in contrast, consists of a number of workers (or collections of workers, each with its own leader) who operate autonomously but nevertheless consciously seek to coordinate their activities. Members are jointly responsible for achieving the network's objectives, though each person takes independent decisions and there is no coherent chain of command. Rather, members are (usually) of equal rank and are accountable to a single central control. Networking is an increasingly popular form of business organisation, particularly when people prefer to work from home (computer software experts for example) and/or when highly specialised professional skills are involved.

Teamwork

A *team* is a special sort of group. All teams are groups, but groups do not necessarily behave as teams. The defining characteristic of a team is that its members cooperate and *voluntarily* coordinate their work in order to achieve group objectives. Team members are highly interdependent and each individual must to some extent interpret the nature of his or her particular role. Members feel especially upset, therefore, when they consider that a colleague has let them down, say by not doing a fair share of the work of the team. In a team, each person feels inwardly responsible for promoting the interests of the working group and personally accountable for its actions. Teams have leaders who may or may not be appointed by an outside body (higher management for example), but the authority of the leader of a team, as distinct from any working group, is fully accepted by all its members. The team leader represents the group to the outside world and is formally answerable for its behaviour. Within a team there will be a high degree of group cohesion, much interaction, mutual support and shared perceptions of issues. Team members will be willing to interchange roles, share workloads and generally help each other out. Typically, each team member will hold other members in high regard and will experience much satisfaction from belonging to the team. A working group can develop into a team and vice versa, a team can lose its coherence and begin to operate as if it were a network (with each member working independently and in emotional isolation from other participants) or as a hierarchy within which individuals will not initiate activity unless they are instructed to do so by a direct superior.

Team spirit is obviously desirable in a working group. To foster team spirit you need consciously to implement a participative management style. Try to adopt the following rules:

- praise and encourage members' suggestions for altering working methods: never be sarcastic about new ideas, no matter how impracticable they might appear. If, in your view, a suggestion stands no chance of success then simply point out its prohibitive cost or other reason for its unacceptability. You could be wrong, so invite discussion on your objections

- clarify territorial divisions among team members. Ensure that all members are fully aware of the extent of their individual and collective responsibilities. Much conflict can arise from petty 'who does what' ambiguities. See to it that formal job specifications correspond to the duties that team members actually undertake

- represent and defend the team in the outside world. Do not criticise members in front of outsiders. As far as possible, back up team members' decisions even when you believe them to be wrong

- fight for resources for staff development and extra training for individuals within your team. Even if you do not succeed, your efforts will be appreciated by team members.

If people have to work well together in order to carry out their individual duties they are more likely to want to cooperate with others and will soon develop a common bond. This is true even if team members are of unequal rank — mutual dependence of higher and lower levels of authority quickly creates a unity of purpose. Other causes of good team spirit are: a fair distribution of work and responsibility within the group, especially of unpleasant or exceptionally demanding tasks; well-designed work programmes with realistic completion dates; compatibility of the personal characteristics of participants.

Self-check

Distinguish between a hierarchy, a network and a team as an approach to organisational structure.

Answer

Hierarchy: pyramid structure, clear chain of command with clearly defined span of control

Network: workers operate autonomously but coordinate activities, no coherent chain of command

Team: voluntary cooperation and coordination, loyal to other members, strong desire to meet the objectives of the group.

If the team's workload is unacceptably demanding (as happens when some members simultaneously fall ill or resign without being immediately replaced) then you must determine priorities and consciously reduce the volume of tasks undertaken. Exclude first those duties that absorb the greatest time and create the least benefit, but take care not to cut out essential tasks simply because they are disliked by members of the team. If you are completely overwhelmed with work, try to isolate a distinct subgroup of activities that can be put together and allocated to another team.

Activity

We would all advocate team spirit as being desirable. Consider the groups under your control for a moment. Which group best illustrates the presence of team spirit and which group best illustrates the absence of team spirit?

Team spirit is difficult to measure but its benefits are clear to see. In the text, several ways of fostering team spirit have been outlined. Perhaps you should try to implement some of them and measure the results.

In situations where team morale suffers through the behaviour of one of the team's members you need to try and alter the behaviour of the person concerned. Recognise, however, that sometimes an individual's conduct and demeanour are so embedded in his or her personality that they will *never* change. Here you must either accept that person as he or she is, or hope that he or she will grow out of the behaviour which is causing difficulties or make arrangements for that person to be transferred to another team. Bad conduct is rarely perceived as such by the person concerned. You need, therefore, not only to draw the deviant member's attention to the undesirable consequences of the bad behaviour but also to break it down into component parts and analyse the causes and effects of each element against the background in which it occurs. Whether behaviour is good or bad often depends on the context of the incident — it is bad to ignore paperwork that is essential for the efficient functioning of the team but good to discard superfluous paperwork that would interfere with more important work. Thus, you ought not to criticise a member for failing to respond to letters and memoranda until you know the full circumstances of the events.

Define precisely the behaviour you believe needs to be altered, and how exactly you would like it to change. List the things the person is currently doing that you would like him or her to stop and all the things the person is not doing that you wish he or she would do. Arrange an interview with the person concerned and during the interview approach the issue circumspectly, focusing your conversation on the *effects* of the undesirable behaviour on the efficiency of the team.

Leading a team

Morale within your team will be enhanced if you know each of its members personally. You should know their names, something about their backgrounds and what they expect to achieve through involvement with the group. Make it known that you welcome initiative, new ideas and independent attempts to solve problems. Consult regularly with individual members and be ready to alter working structures and arrangements following the consultations. Treat subordinates as individuals, be aware of their strengths, weaknesses and potential. Keep everyone informed of the progress of the team and ensure that each member's contribution is fully recognised.

Activity

How well do you know the members of the team you lead?

It is important to know people's names and their work backgrounds. It is especially difficult when you meet people for the first time and it can help to break the ice if you know a little about them. It may be worthwhile keeping a personal record of what you know about each team member.

Participative decision-taking is good for encouraging team spirit. In certain circumstances, however, participation in decisions is not feasible, eg when highly technical and/or specialised matters are involved, or decisions need to be taken so quickly that consultation with subordinates cannot occur. Having taken a decision in such circumstances do not merely impose it on the group, but try instead to persuade the group that you have made the correct choice. Otherwise, try to suggest (rather than impose) solutions to problems. Invite comment and alternative views on issues and seek consensus on a common approach. Make sure that everyone understands the team's decision making procedures and whether responsibility for decisions will rest with you as the appointed leader or, in the case of democratic decisions (based ultimately on votes), with the entire team.

Symptoms of poor teamwork are easily recognised: absenteeism, latecoming, high staff turnover, bad temper, deprecatory remarks about other team members and so on. Staff lose confidence in the team's ability to achieve its objectives, comment is interpreted as criticism, the quality of work declines, staff lack effort and petty grievances arise. When this happens, undertake a complete review of the objectives and activities of the team. Look at physical working conditions, wage levels and relativities, terms and conditions of employment (do the staff feel secure in their jobs, for example) and interpersonal relations within the group. Examine also the status of the group in the hierarchy of the total organisation. Has it sufficient resources? Does senior management appreciate the work the team performs and does management understand the problems it faces? Consider introducing job enrichment programmes and reassess the adequacy of your own leadership style, especially the extent to which you allow subordinates to participate in decisions and act independently.

Self-check

List the symptoms of poor teamwork.

Answer
Symptoms are likely to be similar to those indicating poor motivation. Quantity and quality of work are likely to be affected by poor teamwork but these are unlikely to be the first signs that something is wrong.

Earlier signs are likely to be bad temper among staff, frequent squabbles, absenteeism, poor punctuality and high labour turnover.

Handling conflict

Conflict has positive aspects: it spurs initiative, creates energy and stimulates new ideas. Unfortunately, it can also cause the misdirection of efforts against workmates instead of towards the achievement of the organisation's common goals. Try to analyse systematically the sources of conflicts you experience especially if they concern personal rather than organisational problems.

Usually, conflicts at work arise in one of two categories: conflicts between your function and those of others or conflicts with higher authority or subordinates. To resolve conflicts you might appeal to higher authority to impose solutions, compromise or (assuming you are empowered to do so) impose your own will. The latter encourages retaliation and discourages the free interchange of information and ideas. However, imposed solutions are frequently better than compromises (even if the solutions established are not popular) since compromises satisfy neither party to a dispute.

It is often easier to deal with conflicts between other people than those involving yourself. Third party disputes can be approached objectively and without presumptions and you are better able to identify symptoms of distress. Look for breakdowns in communication and unwarranted arguments between individuals for unnecessary, perhaps even harmful, competition between functions and for inflexible, insensitive attitudes towards other employees. Further indicators of impending conflict are people deliberately withholding information from each other, abuse of colleagues behind their backs, excessively formal relations between individuals and unwarranted criticism of the quality of other peoples' work.

Activity

How do you handle conflict situations at work? Do you have a procedure that you follow or do you improvise?

Conflict situations can be creative or destructive. In the former case, conflict will stimulate new ideas and discussion, whereas in the latter it will involve malice and be dysfunctional.

As a manager, you have to consider each situation on its merits and decide whether and when to intervene. When you do intervene, you must be seen to be fair and the use of a simple checklist may help you. You must identify who is involved, what happened and why. Any solution must tackle the root cause of the problem or it will re-appear at a later date. Ideally, the solution should be acceptable to all parties, but more importantly it must be fair and reasonable.

In seeking to resolve conflicts between colleagues, relate their behaviour to the objectives of the teams to which they belong. Objectives provide solid criteria for decisions when arbitrating disputes. Clarify each person's formal role as specified in the firm's organisation chart or manual and offer interpretations of peoples' roles where opinions differ. Define job boundaries and ask each side to detail *why* they consider the other's behaviour to be unreasonable. Initially you should speak to the disputants individually, but in so doing ask each party to suggest items for the agenda of a meeting to settle the dispute. Ask each side to empathise with the other's position.

Working with a secretary

One vitally important but often neglected example of practical teamwork concerns the working relationship between boss and secretary. Depending on the nature of your work and the organisation of secretarial duties within the firm you might either have your own secretary working entirely within the department, or you might share a secretary with other managers in other departments. Whichever the case, your secretary is your communications link with the rest of the organisation and the outside business world and your working habits have to alter once you acquire a secretary. Two problems commonly arise: inappropriate structuring of secretaries' workloads and unwillingness to recognise the value of secretaries' contributions to the boss/secretary team — some managers with personal secretaries see them as appendages to themselves rather than as important employees in their own right.

Your secretary takes over much of your correspondence and effectively represents you to the outside world, thus creating your public image, an image that might be difficult to live up to and which possibly contradicts your own view of yourself. It is thus essential that you communicate well with each other and have a common understanding of how you will present your joint efforts to others. Together you must agree, perhaps tacitly, on the degree of formality of your relationship and about who will ultimately determine the style and layout of letters, reports and memoranda, bearing in mind that secretaries are invariably better qualified in these respects. Most importantly, you must agree about the way records are to be kept and the diary controlled within the office, and about which aspects of work the secretary is to be free to make independent decisions. Who for example will choose filing systems and other clerical procedures, determine the locations of desks, chairs and cabinets, the deployment of potted plants and so on?

Secretaries should perform those tasks they can do best, which today could involve acting as an information technology specialist, perhaps possessing a higher level of knowledge than the boss! Some supervisors resent this situation. It may not be easy to accept that the person who types letters, does the filing, etc is also capable of operating sophisticated business software that many supervisory managers cannot understand but without which they cannot work effectively. Bosses themselves now need to possess rudimentary keyboarding and software skills otherwise they are not able to function (eg by accessing computer stored data) when their secretaries are away.

Activity

If you have a secretary, what qualifications does this employee possess?

If you cannot list these qualifications, then try to get hold of the information, as without it you may not be making the most of the secretary's abilities.

Qualifications are likely to include shorthand, typing, word processing, office practice. Qualifications might include foreign languages, book-keeping, 'A' levels, degree, business studies, RSA Personal Assistant's Diploma, LCC Personal Secretarial Certificate.

More than ever before, boss and secretary need to work together as a team, which requires that both boss and secretary be able to make and take criticism without causing or perceiving offence. You must take your secretary into your confidence and provide all the information necessary to do the job effectively. It is easy to criticise whilst conveniently forgetting that you have not kept your secretary up-to-date with all the information available on the various projects with which you are involved. If you believe that a secretarial task should be completed in a certain way, then say so before it is finished. Standards should be established from the outset on both sides. If, for example, you are pedantic about the style of layout and typing accuracy of letters leaving the office it is unfair for you to imply that anything less than a high (predetermined) standard is acceptable, only to complain that work has not been completed according to specified standards when it is finished and presented for signature.

Always think twice before asking that work be repeated. Poor typing is a reasonable complaint, as is transcription that significantly alters the meaning of the text, but insistence that transcription *must* be word for word as dictated is unreasonable and unnecessary; it implies that the secretary does not have the ability to transcribe notes properly and/or is not competent to decide when a slight change in wording will improve the style of a document. People interpret tasks differently and so long as the end product is completed to a satisfactory standard within a reasonable time it is irrelevant and extremely annoying for either boss or secretary constantly to give opinions on the other's working methods. This does not mean that a secretary (or a boss) should never be criticised or that working methods should not be discussed, only that such conversations be planned and conducted dispassionately. The best time to do this is normally during periods set aside for dictation or for organising future work.

With the advent of word processing there has arisen a tendency for bosses to redraft work several times on the assumption that little effort is involved in retyping. This is a false assumption: files have to be found, programs loaded and points in the text needing amendment located. Further time is then absorbed in finishing the edit and printing the revised version. Yet in fact, the boss's retrospective feeling that a different wording might have improved the style of a document may have been little more than a passing fancy.

Too often, firms appoint overqualified secretaries to jobs that require only elementary office skills. Bosses frequently imagine there is a special prestige attached to employing a highly qualified person as a secretary, perhaps insisting that the secretary be a graduate and/or have high shorthand/typing speeds or speak several languages. Managers are attracted by high qualifications in candidates for secretarial posts but fail to realise how bored a secretary possessing these high qualifications will feel when asked to perform unskilled clerical tasks. If highly qualified people are used as receptionist/coffee makers with little prospect of applying their knowledge they will quickly look for better jobs.

Self-check

Do you agree with the assumption that little effort is involved in retyping work since the advent of word processing?

Answer
If you agree with this statement, then perhaps you should gain some insight into how the word processor operates. Changes for changes' sake are a waste of everyone's time.

Ask yourself how you would react in a similar situation. Most bosses would not willingly remain long in positions bearing little relation to their job descriptions or which offered negligible opportunities for interesting work. When recruiting a secretary, seriously consider the precise role you wish the secretary to play and the skills levels and knowledge actually needed to perform that role effectively. The aim should be to utilise the strengths of the secretary as well as the strengths of the boss, and to establish rapport and good communications between the two.

You and your secretary must negotiate the secretary's workload. Managers commonly fail to realise that in allocating work to a secretary they are, in effect, structuring their secretaries' working lives. Bosses typically have many contacts and work interests beyond the boss/secretary relationship, yet secretaries are entirely dependent on their bosses for work. A boss who, for example, gives a secretary large amounts of copy typing may not appreciate the intolerable consequences that hour after hour spent before a word processor or the tedium that long uninterrupted periods spent on humdrum work can create. Serious problems occur when bosses become so reliant on good secretaries that they are reluctant to recommend them for promotion. By doing the job well the secretary becomes indispensable and thus can only advance by leaving the organisation! This prospect can frustrate and distress the secretary to such an extent that current performance suffers. It is obviously reasonable that well-qualified secretaries should have career aspirations and view each job as a means of enhancing their experience. Thus you should never interfere with your secretary's promotion prospects — doing so will simply encourage the secretary to resign.

Secretaries with several bosses

An important consequence of the introduction of information technology to the modern office is that today many secretaries work for several bosses. There are obvious advantages to this situation: secretaries are given a greater variety of work, are fully employed, accumulate wider experience, are more likely to use advanced secretarial and other qualifications and the system overcomes the not uncommon problem of secretaries sometimes being hired for their looks and the prestige they bring to a boss rather than for their actual contributions — incompetent secretaries cannot survive long when they have to work for many bosses. Against the system is the difficulty of coordinating the secretary's work and the conflicts of loyalty to various bosses that the situation creates. A one-to-one relationship enables a sort of unwritten boss/secretary contract to exist, so that for example you might tolerate the secretary's occasional absence or frequent latecoming in return for the secretary's willingness to work overtime whenever required. Secretary and boss might take turns to make the tea (bosses should remember that secretaries' time can be just as valuable as theirs at crucial moments) and clear and precise criteria for delineating the decisions the boss shall take from those to be taken by the secretary can be mutually agreed — it is unfair to expect a secretary to take important decisions that should be taken by the boss, even if the boss happens to be out when crucial decisions are required.

Secretaries should always be present when the division of their work is debated, and it is essential that in many-boss situations the various bosses delegate to the one secretary some interesting as well as routine work. Patterns of authority and accountability within the many person team must be defined exactly — secretaries sometimes resent being directly supervised by even a single boss and find the experience of being administered by several bosses completely intolerable, especially when the secretary exercises discretion about how much of each managers' workload to assume. Rules are needed to ensure that conflicting instructions are not issued, and the several bosses must jointly realise that secretaries are *entitled* to job satisfaction. Tasks need to be varied and secretarial jobs enriched (by increasing the importance of decisions taken) and enlarged (through extending the range of the secretary's activities).

7

Solving Problems and Taking Decisions

Objectives

This chapter will help you to:

- adopt a logical and systematic approach to problem-solving and decision-making
- distinguish between strategic, tactical and operational decisions.

Some people seem incapable of acting decisively, and when they do take decisions they are inconsistent, act hastily and do not consider all relevant facts. Prevarication causes muddle and irritates colleagues. Others insist on becoming involved in *all* decisions, regardless of whose responsibilities they ought to be. These people try to solve their colleagues' problems as well as their own — creating confusion, duplication of effort and eventually preventing anything being fully resolved. Yet, all management involves taking decisions, and the calibre of a manager will be judged in large part against his or her decision taking abilities. The need for decisions arises from problems which, in a business context, might be 'strategic' (concerning the overall direction of the firm), 'tactical' (how to *implement* policy decisions) or 'operational' (relating to routine administrative matters such as the lengths of production runs, shift rosters, stock levels etc). Where possible, operational decisions should be taken automatically in accordance with some predetermined decision rule and not require judgement or discretion (automatically replenishing inventories whenever some minimum predetermined stock level is reached, for example).

Top management takes strategic decisions, lower levels are concerned primarily with tactical decision taking and control. Supervisors do not normally take policy decisions. If they do, they are not classified as 'supervisors' but as occupants of higher managerial positions. To take decisions effectively, you need to analyse systematically the steps involved in decision taking and assess critically the criteria on which you base decisions. Often, decisions do not justify careful thought. The best choice might be obvious, or the consequences of a bad decision may be so trivial that little attention is required. For big decisions, however, you need to think hard and long not only about the issue but also about the manner in which your decision will be reached. You must analyse the various courses of action available to you, their likely consequences and the probabilities of certain events. Information must be gathered, viable options listed, and their implications assessed.

Self-check

Distinguish between strategic, tactical and operational decisions.

Answer

Strategic decisions — relate to the overall direction and policy of the organisation, and as such are confined to the most senior levels of management.

Tactical decisions — are concerned with how to achieve the policy objectives and can involve lower levels of management.

Operational decisions — are concerned with daily routine matters, minor adjustments as they relate to tactical decisions. Floor managers and supervisory grades will be directly involved in this area.

Predetermined strategies for solving problems can usually be applied, provided you analyse carefully the nature of the problem and the environment in which it arose. Some decisions (the recruitment of new staff for instance) are best taken by more than one person, and most significant decisions are improved through consultation with those who will be affected by them. List in order of importance the major decisions you expect to have to take in the foreseeable future, but do not necessarily tackle them in this order. Routine 'maintenance' decisions (work allocations, production scheduling, office lay-out, etc) might conveniently be dealt with together on (say) a single predetermined afternoon. Other decisions may need more time to prepare and should therefore be deferred until all the necessary data is assembled. Keep a record of the *sources* of major problems. It could be that certain individuals, events or departments cause more problems than others.

Decision taking processes

Several algorithms have been devised for taking decisions. Most are based on the work of the mathematician GA Polya who (in the context of solving mathematical problems) suggested a four-fold scheme: analysis of the problem, consideration of auxiliary problems, planning a solution, and implementing and monitoring the chosen course of action.[1]

Analysis of the problem

Do not be pressurised into taking snap decisions on important issues without properly analysing the problem. Write out a formal definition of what exactly you need to decide. Specify the problem as carefully and in as much detail as possible, ensuring that no relevant facts are left out.

What is the true nature of the problem? Is it technical, financial, personal, or a mixture of these? Is the problem self-contained, or is it a manifestation of an underlying malaise? If the real problem is deep rooted, what are its *fundamental* causes? Collect and examine all the available facts. Determine which information is based on hard evidence and which on speculation, and specify any additional information you will need.

It is essential that problems be clearly and precisely defined: misstatements of the problems result in inappropriate solutions being applied. For example, the problem of reducing your departmental expenditure might be interpreted as either how to reduce (say) stationery costs, or how to increase efficiency, or as a redundancy problem involving the choice of personnel to be sacked! So before committing yourself to a formal definition, look at the problem from several points of view.

Planning a solution

Often, major problems consist of a conglomeration of lesser, interrelated problems. Dissect large problems into their constituent parts and deal with each part as if it were a separate problem. Prepare a list of the resources necessary to implement a successful solution, and compare these with the resources available. Specify the environmental conditions that must remain constant for your plans to work and consider *all* possible solutions to the problem — not just some of them. If you rely on subordinates' reports for ideas on feasible solutions, ensure they do not withhold from you one or two viable options they do not wish to see implemented and the existences of which they thus conceal.

List the people who will be involved in the chosen solution and its implementation and give them the information they need, ensuring that each person receives the information in an understandable and readily digestible form. Do your colleagues agree about who should take particular decisions; and if not why? Ask for views on issues — consult people in advance rather than simply informing them after decisions have been taken. However, only consult individuals whose views are directly relevant to the issue and/or will be personally affected by the decision — much time can be wasted in meaningless consultations with people who are only marginally interested in a problem. Normally, the range of individuals consulted and the length of time spent gathering and analysing information depends on the significance of the decision to be taken and the consequences of the decision being wrong, though in some cases there will simply not be enough time to consult everyone who could be involved.

Next, identify the barriers that might prevent a satisfactory outcome. Outline the best possible solution to the problem, and then prepare two lists of restricting factors, the first containing

---

Self-check

Why is it essential to analyse the problem before looking for possible solutions?

Answer

A careful analysis of the problem itself is a prerequisite for identifying the best solution. This first stage is so obvious that it is frequently rushed. Failure to define the problem accurately will result in inappropriate solutions, which will not resolve the problem.

(endogenous) items that you can control and the second specifying exogenous factors, entirely beyond your influence. Put down every constraint that occurs to you, regardless of how trivial it might at first appear (you can edit later) and, for endogenous items, write a brief account of how each barrier might be overcome and what resources (human, technical and financial) will be needed for achieving this.

Decisions that require critical judgement are usually based on one of three criteria: experience, experimentation, or research:

- Experienced managers bring breadth of knowledge and background information to their decision making roles. Of course, experience needs to be relevant and up to date, it is no substitute for technical ability or professional expertise. Experience, moreover, relates to past events whereas current decisions affect the future.

- Experimentation is sometimes possible in business situations. For example, organisational structures within a firm might be manipulated and their effects observed. The problem with experiments is that they occur under highly specific conditions, which might not be repeatable or continue in the future and human behaviour can be highly inconsistent and hence unpredictable even within a laboratory environment.

- Research covers many activities including collection and analysis of information, procedures for generating new ideas, speculative investigation, or application of advanced modelling techniques. Usually, research is most useful where variables affecting the decision are tangible and can be accurately measured.

Brainstorming

If you are stuck for ideas you can *brainstorm* a problem, individually or with colleagues. The aim is to churn out ideas without considering their feasibility. You simply list every idea on any aspect of the problem that comes into your head. Then, in another session, you go through the list of ideas assessing whether they are sensible, practicable, within your available resources etc. Be as inventive and imaginative as you can; look at the problem from different angles instead of head-on. You will find that one idea generates others and that ideas build on themselves.

Group brainstorming sessions are useful only if participants take them seriously and are competent to contribute fresh ideas about the problem. However, members should *never* be criticised for suggesting (superficially) absurd or trivial ideas and there should be no discussion of ideas at this stage. Write the ideas on a blackboard or flip chart as they arise and keep a permanent record of the items suggested. Then convene a *separate* meeting to evaluate the ideas. Keep a record of the justifications for removing items you subsequently deem unacceptable. List the benefits, costs and implications of each idea that survives vetting and choose the best option.

Brainstorming results in new ideas and perspectives that would never otherwise emerge. Consider for example the problem of overcoming persistent unjustified absenteeism among employees. A 10 minute brainstorm might produce (among many others) the list of points shown in Example 4.1.

Next you order the points according to their importance and feasibility. Collect together all similar items, with each 'section' of ideas containing no more than half a dozen entries. Allocate a sub-heading to each section, and alongside specify its relationship to the problem. Organise the sub-headings in order of their relevance and begin to 'fill-out' the points. As your ideas develop, list the difficulties, constraints, resource requirements etc associated with each, again placing these in a logical order. Finish the brainstorm within a predetermined period,

Example 4.1

Absenteeism and oversleeping
Age and absenteeism
Pregnancy
Legal aspects of
  absenteeism
Absenteeism and:
  alcohol
  drug abuse
  illness
  working conditions
  leisure
  public transport
  neighbours
  sex
Trade unions and absenteeism
The government and absenteeism
Effects on the economy
Looking after children
Lost wages
Social security and absenteeism
Effects on workgroups
Letting down colleagues
Social interactions
The history of absenteeism
New working hours
Covering up for colleagues
Absenteeism in:
  other firms
  other industries
  other cities
  other countries
Politics and absenteeism
Examples set by senior
  managers
Visibility of absent colleagues
Corruption and absenteeism
Teenagers and absenteeism
Accidents

Morale and absenteeism
Approaching retirement
Travel problems
Costs of absenteeism
Benefits of absenteeism
Disciplinary considerations
Absenteeism among top
  managers
Poor working conditions and
  absenteeism
Workers' attitudes towards
  absenteeism
Wages and absenteeism
The future of absenteeism
What workers do when they
  are absent
Wives, husbands and children
  and absenteeism
Women and absenteeism
Absenteeism in schools
Shopping
Dismissal
Suspensions
Job sharing
Absenteeism as a protest
Recording absenteeism
Shiftwork
Council houses and absenteeism
Home repairs
Home decorating
Summer and absenteeism
Christmas and absenteeism
Corporate image of the
  firm
Social standing and authority
  of supervisors
Job rotation
Part time working

seeking always to convert ideas into coherent and viable *action plans*.

Auxiliary problems

Problems similar to those currently being experienced might have appeared before but in a different form. If so, examine the consequences of the previous solution, since even if a particular problem has not previously appeared, a related or similar problem may have been settled. Solutions to kindred problems offer hints on how best to tackle the problem in question. Sometimes, problems can be restated to make them resemble other problems previously encountered. Aim to discover what a problem is about — what its *fundamental* nature involves. Try to think of several possible manifestations of the problem and how each one might be tackled. How did the problem arise? Is it caused by fresh circumstances, or can difficulties common to several problems be discerned?

Implementation

The selected solution should be made known to all affected parties and an action plan with dates, specific targets and detailed work allocations devised to ensure its implementation. Then, the effectiveness of the solution must be monitored and remedial action taken if it does not produce the desired results. If you have chosen to do nothing about a particular problem you should still monitor the situation to check whether the problem has 'cured itself' or whether further difficulties have emerged.

Decisions are useless unless they are carried out. Ensure, therefore, that those selected to implement a decision not only understand it and what they must do, but also are committed to the decision and will not seek to undermine the intended outcome. It is thus useful if the people who took the decision are themselves involved in its enforcement and where possible the activities needed to implement a decision should follow from clear directives issued at the moment the decision was made. These directives should not be open to interpretation and should be executed by predetermined dates. Some named person should be made responsible for implementing each aspect of the decision. Choice of the personnel to undertake these duties and the establishment of a timetable might themselves represent important decisions.

Difficulties arise when the decision taker is unsure about what he or she expects from a decision, so always specify clearly the positive changes you anticipate following your action and check to ensure that further problems are not created by these changes.

Monitor the effectiveness of the solution selected. Maintain careful records so that this solution can be used to solve similar problems which subsequently arise.

Risk

Risk is involved in many management decisions and the existence of risk sometimes causes supervisors to avoid or delay taking decisions in risky situations. The size of the risk must be compared with the expected benefits of a particular decision.

Self-check

Why is it necessary to monitor the effectiveness of the solution selected?

Answer

There is no guarantee that, having implemented the solution, the desired results will be achieved ie the problem is resolved. There may be a myriad of reasons for the lack of success, including bad luck, bad timing, poor implementation, poor solution. Essentially, the decision-making process starts all over again.

Low-risk high-return solutions are obviously preferable to high-risk low-return options. Typically, however, a compromise between risk and return has to be struck and the precise nature of the compromise will depend largely on the risk preferences of the person taking the decision. Some people enjoy assuming risk, others are highly averse to risky behaviour. Indeed, a few individuals find risk so exciting that they are prepared to forego satisfactory outcomes just to experience the exhilaration it provides.

You might 'take a risk' by hiring someone not seemingly suited to a particular job, by accepting a tight delivery date for a consignment of goods you know might not be ready on time, by making promises you cannot guarantee to keep or by accepting someone else's promise when you know it might be broken. At what point does risky behaviour become irresponsible? Where do you draw the line between risk and potential return? A fondness for excitement and tendency to act on impulse can cause you to behave recklessly, so always prepare a brief analysis of the risks involved in an important decision, and cover yourself by involving other people in risky choices. (If you are an exceptionally risk averse person you might find you are more willing to select high risk options when the decision is shared by a group.) Also, specify the minimum probabilities of success required of each option: this will help you avoid rash behaviour and *consciously* to decide whether a risk is worth taking.

Note

1 Polya, GA, *How to solve It*, Princeton University Press, Princeton, New Jersey, 1945.

8
Planning

Objectives

This chapter will help you to:

- understand the need for a systematic approach to planning
- become familiar with the concept of corporate planning.

Planning means deciding now what to do in the future given certain predicted or intended conditions. It requires the analysis of present circumstances, precise definition of objectives and the design of strategies and tactics for achieving targets. Planning is troublesome and expensive, troublesome because it requires forecasts of the future, expensive because it absorbs large amounts of time. Nevertheless, planning is invariably worthwhile. It forces you to prepare for unforeseen eventualities, to clarify your objectives, to develop criteria for monitoring performance and to think ahead systematically. Also, it demands the conscious coordination of projects and the active participation and cooperation of subordinates and other colleagues in the formation and execution of planned activities. The manager who plans ahead is better equipped to accommodate change. Moreover, the planning process itself might:

- identify opportunities for greater efficiency
- reveal duplications of effort, bottlenecks in workflows and foreseeable pitfalls

- indicate fresh initiatives that the firm might undertake in order to influence future events
- assist in integrating activities.

Planning enables you to take decisions unhurriedly, using the maximum amount of information and considering all available options. This avoids decision making in crisis situations which prevent you studying all relevant factors in depth.

There are three basic approaches to planning: 'top-down' planning, which means that senior management plans and establishes targets for *all* levels of authority within the firm, 'bottom-up' planning, whereby each department prepares an estimate of what it believes it can achieve and submits this to higher management for approval, and a third (and common) method whereby senior management imposes general objectives, leaving individual departments to devise plans for attaining them. Whichever method is adopted, the first stage in a planning process is the specification of objectives, ie, statements of what you want to do (as opposed to 'policies', which state how objectives are to be achieved). The more concrete your objectives the easier the choice of policies needed to attain them. Higher level targets are subdivided into specific objectives (preferably expressed in quantitative terms) to be achieved within predetermined periods.

Forecasts might be needed before targets can be set. A forecast is a prediction of future events, in contrast to a 'plan' which is a predetermined response to anticipated future events. Forecasting is an essential prerequisite to effective planning but, in management, accurate forecasts are (notoriously) difficult to achieve. Environmental change can occur quickly — production techniques become obsolete, employment and other laws alter, new agreements are negotiated with unions. Usually, the shorter the forecast period the more accurate its predictions.

Long term forecasts are subject to greater uncertainty, so larger margins of error must be allowed. Thus, many firms prepare both short and long term forecasts, the former in detail, the latter in outline only. It is not worth spending enormous amounts of money on long range predictions of highly uncertain events. The accuracy of predictions should be monitored by comparing them with events as they occur and

---

Self-check

What three approaches to planning are given in the text?

Answer

Top-down: where the process is restricted to senior levels of management

Bottom-up: where departments submit plans for approval of senior levels

Compromise: where senior levels decide on the overall direction of the organisation and impose objectives for departments, leaving the latter free to decide on how to achieve them.

   You are most likely to find methods 1 and 3 used in your own organisation.

---

sources of error (inadequate or incorrect data, faulty forecasting techniques, poor judgements by forecasters etc) identified to find out whether forecasts are on average persistently over-estimating or underestimating actual performance. Forecasting is considered in great detail later in the chapter.

In practice, top down planning is more common than bottom up planning. The major point in its favour is the inexperience of supervisors and junior managers in policy making. Another drawback to bottom up procedures is that subordinates might not be familiar with the work of other departments, hence their judgements may be short sighted and might conflict with the needs of other aspects of the organisation.

Plans should be as detailed as expenditure constraints allow, but should not extend too far into the future since accurate prediction of the distant future is impossible. All alternative courses of action should be considered, not just some of them and the side effects and implications of the actions envisaged should be examined. Instructions to individuals and departments must be incorporated into the body of the plan. What is the point of preparing an expensive and detailed plan if no-one assumes responsibility for its implementation? As the plan is executed its effectiveness in achieving stated objectives must be monitored and this will be facilitated if the plan is concise and easy to understand. It is essential, moreover, that a comprehensive two way flow of information exist between those who drafted the plan and those who carry it into effect. Note the importance of setting reasonable initial targets; overambitious objectives lead to disillusion and cynicism when they are not achieved. Equally, targets that are too low have little operational significance. Good quality feedback is crucial, therefore, to the success of a plan. Unless there is a mechanism for relating plans to actual performance much of the effort that goes into their formulation is wasted.

The departmental plan

When preparing a departmental plan, analyse systematically the strengths and weaknesses of yourself, the department and your subordinates. Does the department possess all the skills, equipment and human and other resources needed to attain targets? Specify your objectives as precisely as you can and list all the activities necessary to achieve them. Evaluate the consequences of various courses of action and choose the best. Then prepare a list of all the instructions you need to issue to subordinates to secure implementation of the plan and establish criteria (preferably quantitative) for monitoring progress. Do not be afraid to seek advice from subordinates (who often will possess intimate knowledge of day-to-day operations) since it is only fair and reasonable that those required to implement plans participate actively in their formulation. Involvement in the specification of targets motivates individuals towards achievement of the objectives set.

Each plan should be accompanied by a programme for action, specifying what is to be done, when, by whom and how work is to be executed.

Corporate strategy

At the corporate level (or at the very highest level of management in non-corporate organisations) planning focuses primarily on the determination of long range strategies for achieving broadly defined objectives. In deciding their objectives, many firms find it useful to ask three fundamental questions: 'What business are we in?', 'What business do we want to be in?', and 'What do we have to do to get where we want to be?'. Careful analysis of the answers to these questions can indicate whether the firm should diversify its product range, enter new markets, change its price policy, alter existing distribution channels etc.

Strategies may be devised by a single person (the owner of the business, for example) or by a committee such as the board of directors of a limited company. A corporate strategy has two elements: a statement (sometimes referred to as a 'mission statement') about the organisation's purpose, and a statement about the means the organisation intends to adopt in order to achieve its aims. The mission statement will set out the *raison d'être* of the firm, and specify senior management's perception of its role in the wider community. It is a precise statement of why the business exists and where senior management believes the firm should be heading. In preparing a corporate strategy, management must analyse the strengths and weaknesses of the business and the opportunities and threats it faces. Strengths and weaknesses can be specified in relation to existing plant and equipment, the adequacy of labour and supplies, access to finance, product range and quality and so on. Opportunities and threats usually originate outside the firm — in the emergence of new technologies, new competitors, changes in government or in public taste or in possibilities for entering new and untested markets.

There are two basic approaches to corporate strategy, either to identify the activities the business does (or could do) really well and concentrate on these, or to seek new opportunities in entirely different fields. The former course assumes the firm can continue its current activities without hindrance and at peak efficiency, ie it assumes that no significant threats from competitors, poor industrial relations, interruptions in supplies, or impending technological developments, currently exist. For the second option, realistic opportunities have to be available and the firm must possess some means for their identification. Thus, the organisation might initiate an internal research and development programme, undertake market research, monitor economic trends, and so on.

Devising a corporate strategy

A common starting point for drafting a corporate strategy is for the firm to ask itself certain sets of questions. The first of these relate to the industry in which the firm operates. What is the current rate of technical change in the industry? How might this alter? What does the company need to do to beat its rivals in the technical field? Firms in fast changing high-tech industries, for example, may need to invest heavily in product research and development, even at the expense of other activities. How does the company's output differ from that of competitors and what should it do to take full advantage of these differences when marketing its products? Should the firm devote more of its resources to design rather than (say) distribution? Is the company's access to raw materials and skilled labour assured and if not what can be done to improve the situation (eg by offering higher wages or raw materials prices in order to secure continuing supply)?

Strategy formulation must be tackled in the widest context possible. When specifying objectives for example, it is not sufficient merely to list those options which relate to *current* activities. Rather, the firm must consider the feasibility of radical changes to its product, markets and production methods — to move, perhaps, from engineering to computers, from textiles to pottery, or from transport to the provision of retailing services. The question is not so much 'How can we improve our current operations?' but 'What *else* can we do in order to maximise our profits and growth?'. Answers might suggest a diversification strategy — new products, new markets and/or the adoption of new technologies — or a strategy of consolidation of existing market share, seeking perhaps to improve profitability through disinvestment in unprofitable activities and/or the acquisition of other firms.

Stated corporate objectives are not necessarily capable of being achieved. For example, a firm may state that it wishes to dominate a particular market, knowing full well that were it to achieve this the government would intervene via anti-monopoly legislation. Yet the *attempt* to dominate the market might itself be highly profitable and otherwise worthwhile, eg through the acquisition of experience of new methods of marketing and management control.

Corporate strategies and corporate plans

Corporate planning focuses on strategic issues, though some tactical and operational aspects of management are necessarily involved. A good corporate plan will facilitate the coordination of activities, assist in the allocation of resources and increase the organisation's ability to cope with change. Thus, corporate planning concerns the *total* resources and intended activities of the firm. Above all, it is about the management of change — new methods, materials, skills, processes and techniques — and the consideration of the effects of change lies at the heart of the corporate planning process. Corporate plans cover all aspects of the firm's operations: personnel, finance, production, organisation, marketing, management and control.

A corporate plan offers guidelines against which the performance of the organisation may be assessed. It is analogous to a route map showing the direction in which the organisation should proceed. Corporate plans rarely extend to more than four or five years ahead, because of the great uncertainty of long term predictions: few organisations would claim to possess information systems capable of looking more than five years into the future. The plan will describe the activities and resources needed for intended future operations, identifying possible new markets, applications of new technology and the likelihood of environmental change.

Plans could establish corporate targets for (say) the market share to be achieved within three years, a certain rate of return on capital employed, some specified percentage reduction in the labour force, greater efficiency in the use of working capital, lower aggregate expenditures and so on. Achievement of these aims may require new investment or divestment, mergers and acquisitions, new product development or entry to new markets.

Objectives can be listed in order of importance and hence

Activity

Corporate planning is really a continuous cycle of events and can be depicted by a diagram. Without referring to the text, draw your own diagram.

Below you will find a suggested outline. Do not worry if you have more or less stages, or if you have used different terminology.

Figure 6.2

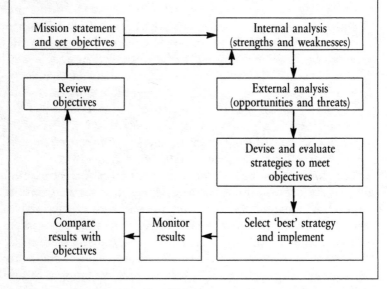

priorities assigned to the policies (and resources) needed for their attainment. Each element of the corporate plan should have a direct and recognisable connection with the statement of the organisation's *raison d'être*. The financial, personnel, technical and other resources necessary to implement the plan must be listed and compared with the resources available and stated deficiencies accompanied by a written explanation of how the shortfall will be met (and who will be responsible for this). The plan should set priorities for action, describe any changes in organisation structure that might be required and include a timetable for its implementation. Then the minimum criteria that need to be satisfied before the plan can be regarded as a 'success' must be specified (eg quantitative targets for improvements in market share, reduced costs, or increased financial return over some predetermined period). The specification of plans requires a critical appraisal of both external and internal factors.

Activity

Does your organisation have a corporate plan? If so, you may find it useful to find out more about it, such as who was involved, how it was drawn up, the time span etc.

External (environmental) factors

External forces can cause strategies to change. A technological development, for example, may devastate an industry. Consider for instance the changeover from conventional typewriting to word processing. Firms producing ordinary typewriters were, in a limited sense, in the same industry as the manufacturers of WPs (ie the creation of letters, memoranda, reports and other 'hard copy' documents) but the skills of their employees and their processes of manufacture were essentially 'mechanical' in orientation. They made and assembled typing keys, roller bars etc and were not in a position to transfer these engineering skills to the computer based technologies that word processing involves (microelectronics, computer programming, software design and so on). Even the materials from which WPs are constructed (circuit boards, microchips, plastic keyboards) are different to those in a typewriter.

Yet the accurate prediction of future technological (and market) environments is extremely difficult. Not all environmental factors can be investigated (there are simply too many of them) so a handful of seemingly relevant external variables must be selected for research.

Activity

In the planning process, organisations must be alive to the environment in which they operate and try to identify opportunities and threats that exist or are likely to arise in the future.

Try to identify as many external factors that might influence your organisation as you can. At this stage, do not worry about putting them under headings, try out some brainstorming.

Now that you have your list continue to work through the chapter. The next section contains an attempt to categorise the factors.

Normally, these variables will concern:

marketing: the activities of competitors, trends in consumer taste and behaviour, changes in the size and structure of the market, gaps in the market

legislation: government attitudes to the industry, impending statutes, licensing arrangements, possibilities of increased control, taxation, health and safety legislation

technology: production methods and their efficiency, new inventions, materials, processes and costs.

There are two ways of planning for environmental change, also referred to as 'environmental scanning'. The first is to predict the external changes that might occur and then detail how the organisation would be affected by them and how the organisation should respond. Alternatively, the planner may begin with a list of the firm's functions, followed by a listing of all the environmental factors that might affect these functions. The latter course is usually the easier of the two since it is concrete and named individuals can be made responsible for listing relevant factors in each functional department. However, some important variables may be overlooked.

Environmental scanning seeks to identify the opportunities offered by changes in the environment and the threats posed by external change. The problem, of course, is the huge number of potentially relevant environmental variables that exist. In order to narrow down the range of variables it should consider the firm needs to ask itself a long series of 'What would happen if . . .' questions. Thus, it should assess the *consequences* of alterations in various laws, market structures, business practices etc.

Activity

Now that you have a better idea of the sort of factors you might have included in the previous activity, spend a few minutes going through your list and making any amendments you feel necessary.

Internal factors

Internal appraisals seek to evaluate the feasibility of plans in terms of the organisation's ability to implement them using current or anticipated resources. Each of the firm's major functions is examined in turn, and the departments involved are questioned about their activities. The following questions are particularly relevant:

- are the firm's management information systems, forecasting procedures, means of coordinating activity and general administration capable of supporting the policies needed to implement plans and if not — why not
- how adequate are marketing and product research for the specified tasks
- does the firm possess a reliable materials procurement system
- what measures exist for ascertaining when existing products have reached the ends of their life cycles
- has the firm an organisation development programme capable of effecting structural change and if so how long will structural alterations take to implement
- what mechanisms exist for controlling expenditures
- how adequate is the company's human resource plan?

Marketing plans should be examined in respect of product, price, promotional and distribution policies. Products, in particular, will be scrutinised *vis-á-vis* their consumer appeal, production cost and quality (decisions to vary the quality of output have many strategic implications). The firm's ability to finance its intended future operations obviously needs investigation. Thus, trends in working capital and in key financial ratios (profit to sales, the current ratio, stock turn-over, debtors to creditors, etc.) must be examined. On the manufacturing side, plant productivity, machine and warehouse capacities, the availabilities of skilled labour and the efficiency of existing scheduling procedures must be investigated. The effectiveness of the company's administrative methods and the calibre of its management should also be analysed.

Forecasting

All forecasting is difficult, business forecasting (notably sales forecasting) particularly so. Political and legal superstructures can change overnight, taxes can alter and consumer tastes can alter suddenly and in seemingly unpredictable ways. Competing firms may change their prices, new firms might enter the market, new production techniques could become available which require complete reestimation of future output constraints. Note, moreover, that forecasts are usually based on experience of the past and there is no guarantee that past trends or environments will continue.

Probably the most important of all business forecasts is that of future sales, since this will indicate anticipated revenues and determine current purchases of raw materials and levels of employment of the labour (and other resources) needed to produce the goods. Expenditures on inputs are incurred now, but revenues are not realised until later. Therefore, finance is needed to bridge the gap and the firm must borrow to meet its short term expenditure obligations. Contracts are signed and must be honoured even if expected sales do not materialise. Forecasts themselves are normally based on past sales, with appropriate allowances for expected consumer reactions to advertising campaigns, predicted behaviour of competitors,

Activity

You should have two lists, one giving the strengths and weaknesses of the organisation and the other the environmental opportunities and threats. Now it is time to combine the two.

Try to think of as many ways as possible in which the organisation might build on its strengths to take advantage of opportunities. Also, what action can it take to prepare for threats and overcome weaknesses.

Remember, at this stage you are not assessing the feasibility of the proposals, that would be done later.

likely changes in consumer incomes and so on. Obviously, sales forecasting is difficult because there are so many uncontrollable variables involved. It is sensible, therefore, to register several forecasts, each contingent on the occurrence of particular events. Then the firm can decide today how it will react to future environmental changes such as price cuts by competitors, tax alterations or changes in fashion.

Long range forecasting

A long range forecast is as much an act of faith as a statistical prediction — it is a statement of intent, not a prognostication. Plans extending over several years will never be realised unless positive measures (human resource policies, management by objectives procedures, new product development, management training etc) are initiated to secure their achievement. Yet because of the numerous and severe difficulties necessarily attached to long term planning and forecasting and the uncertainty of the benefits likely to result from the exercise, these matters are frequently overlooked. Management becomes preoccupied with shorter term problems and ignores the need to consider longer term issues.

To overcome this problem, some organisations deliberately constitute 'policy committees' to prepare long range forecasts and plans and to inaugurate the policies needed to achieve long run objectives. Such committees meet periodically to speculate about the future. Their membership usually consists of senior managers who are not concerned with routine company administration but rather with diagnostic and organisational activities. Hopefully, such individuals will possess broad outlooks and be able to assess objectively the future prospects of the company. Policy committees might then be able to make valuable inputs to *future* corporate strategy statements since they will already have carefully considered the key variables affecting the business' survival and profitability in the longer term.

Long range forecasts are quantified in general terms, eg expected rate of return on capital employed resulting from successful implementation of strategic policies such as increasing market share, diversification, or the introduction of new technology. There are two basic approaches to long range forecasting.

Gap analysis
The planner sets targets based on what he or she believes to be attainable in the longer term and then compares these targets with forecasts of future achievement taken from projections of current activities — assuming that present circumstances continue. Divergences are then analysed and measures implemented to bridge the gaps.

'What if' analysis
Planners ask a series of questions to establish the various outcomes likely to result from different future environments. Outcomes are quantified in terms of expected sales, costs, expenditures, asset structures, flows of funds and other operational variables. Numerous assumptions are made when forecasting the distant future (three years is a long time in a fast changing business world). It might be assumed, for example, that industrial relations within the firm will remain satisfactory, or that existing suppliers will continue in business, or that distribution networks will still be available in several years' time and many important assumptions about the national (indeed the international) economy have to be stated.

Benefits of corporate planning

A firm with a corporate plan is better equipped to face up to change and hence to profit from new opportunities. Large businesses should find that coordination between divisions and subsidiaries is enhanced, that resources are allocated more efficiently and that product policy — particularly product choice — is improved. Companies which prepare corporate plans can monitor their actual rates of growth (or decline) against predetermined standards, and can arrange their operations coherently and without one activity conflicting with others.

Operational plans are derived from the aggregate corporate plan, which provides a strategic framework within which tactics for achieving the global objectives specified at the corporate level may be devised. Operations can be varied as the plan is implemented according to feedback received and/or as environments alter.

Problems in corporate planning

Many senior managers are unable to cope with the volume and complexity of the information generated in corporate planning processes. They receive so much information in such diverse forms (sales forecasts, written reports, efficiency audits, bar charts, Lorenz curves, statistical analyses etc) that they cannot identify clear priorities for action. The quality of information may be suspect and the system for providing it might be extremely expensive.

A major problem in devising strategic plans for a large company is that very often their successful implementation depends crucially on the success of the organisation's research and development activities. Thus, it might be assumed (perhaps overoptimistically) that a new product will be successfully marketed, or that an efficiency improvement exercise will achieve some predetermined cost saving, or that production research will result in new processes or materials. Thereafter, the entire plan rests on these assumptions and no contingencies are available as and when a critical element fails. Flexibility needs to be woven into the master strategy, with a variety of fallback options ready for quick implementation.

Corporate plans may be *too* successful. Thus, a plan to revolutionise the technology of a certain process might be brilliantly executed, but force the initiating firm into bankruptcy through the business' inability to finance the re-equipping of production lines necessary to implement the new methods (which competitors quickly copy). Equally, the introduction of a completely new product to a market creates opportunities for the firm's competitors to follow its lead, but more efficiently since competitors will have been able to observe and learn from the initiating company's mistakes.

Operational planning

This covers a wide range of activities: scheduling, specification of materials inputs and quality standards, ensuring the compatibility of components etc. Planning enables you to regulate flows of work and minimise interruptions, since you will have already predicted the availabilities of equipment, labour and materials and (hopefully) will have allowed for break-downs, absences of personnel, stock shortages, late deliveries of supplies and so on in your calculations. Your plans should reveal how much work is to be done at various times, where and how it will be done and what resources are available and needed.

Self-check

Identify two benefits and two problems of corporate planning.

Answer
Benefits might include improved coordination between departments, efficient use of resources, monitor performance and compare actual results with targets set, unity of objectives.

Problems might include lack of commitment to the process, lack of reliable information, excessive amounts of information, lack of skill in interpreting information, lack of flexibility, time consuming process.

'Planned maintenance' (PM) means drafting a predetermined programme for the upkeep of equipment and/or buildings. Items are serviced at specified intervals, or whenever certain danger signals appear. The aim is to prevent unanticipated breakdowns through ensuring that equipment or buildings are kept in a satisfactory state of repair. To implement a PM programme you must devise and complete a comprehensive register of all the department's equipment and other property that requires maintenance, its location, condition and age. Then you estimate when and why equipment will break down. This information should be available from past records (details of all breakdowns should be recorded diligently) or from manufacturers' predictions of operating life. It might be worthwhile replacing various items at preset intervals even though they are still operational (as for example when servicing a motor car) in order to avoid the costs and inconveniences of special replacement when failure eventually occurs. The exception is when the time to breakdown is unreliable and the cost of periodic maintenance outweighs that of ad-hoc attention.

Regular inspection is an essential ingredient of planned maintenance, so be sure to draft a timetable for inspecting PM register items and to keep to the timetable even though you have other things to do — routine inspections are often put aside when they interfere with busy schedules. When inspecting equipment, look for known indicators of likely failure (excessive wearing of parts, materials fatigue, changes in shape or colour) and develop a system for identifying such factors. Each time an item fails, take a note of the cause of failure and of the outward signs of its poor condition.

Stores procedures

So much working capital is tied up in stocks of inputs, work-in-progress and finished goods that efficient stock management — storage, movement, record keeping, prevention of pilfering or natural wastage — can create big cost savings for the firm. Stock, remember, has an opportunity cost. It is an idle asset; money not embodied in inventory could have been used to generate extra profits, or (at worst) invested to earn interest.

Self-check

What is the difference between corporate planning and operational planning?

Answer

Corporate planning is undertaken by top level management and is concerned with the total resources and overall direction of the organisation.

Operational planning is more concerned with the day-to-day running of departments, such as ensuring adequate supply of raw materials, maintenance of equipment. It is likely to involve lower management grades, including supervisors.

Stores may be centralised or decentralised. A centralised storage system has the advantage that specialist staff may be employed who can quickly locate requisitioned items and who might even be able to suggest alternatives to currently used components or raw materials. Procedures can be standardised, so that forms and activities will not be duplicated and periodic checking of inventory levels is possible. Central warehouses can be laid out in the most efficient ways. Note also that a single warehouse is more secure than several storage points; fewer security guards are needed since security activities (patrolling, barring of windows, burglar alarms etc) may be concentrated in the one area. However, centralisation requires user departments to collect their supplies from a store which might be geographically remote, and fires or floods in the central warehouse could destroy a firm's entire inventory. Sometimes, therefore, the materials constantly consumed by a department are stored in the department, leaving less frequently requisitioned items with the central warehouse.

A central store should be close to user departments yet easily accessible to outside suppliers who need to unload their goods. The central store might have branches close to user departments. Storekeeping is sometimes the responsibility of the firm's purchasing department, otherwise it comes under production control (on the grounds that those in charge of producing the finished output should manage material inputs). Whichever option is adopted it is important that procedures be unified, consistent, easy to operate and fully integrated into the overall work of the firm.

Storekeeping duties include the maintenance of accurate records on materials entering or leaving the store, periodic stocktaking, security, monitoring inventory levels and requisitioning fresh supplies when stocks are low. An important task is to plan stores layout to ensure fast location of needed items. Accordingly, the warehouse should be split into separate areas for various product types and user departments, with bins and shelves clearly numbered. Items in the greatest demand should be most accessible. Gangways need to be kept unblocked, and traffic flows plainly indicated by painted lines and arrows. Circular traffic flows are preferable to those involving sharp corners.

In the past, stocktaking was usually undertaken annually. Today, however, computerised systems enable the continuous monitoring of stock. Moreover, computerisation has reduced the incidence of clerical errors in stock records. Continuous monitoring using a computer is obviously much cheaper than traditional labour intensive stocktaking methods. Accuracy in stockholding records is essential for effective operational control and for auditing.

Activity

All organisations carry stores and it makes good business sense to manage stock efficiently. Try to find the answers to the following questions:

— are the stores centralised or decentralised
— how are items stored
— who has access to storerooms
— what is the procedure for accessing stores
— how frequently is the stock checked
— what method is used to value stock?

Keep the information to hand as you continue to work through the chapter.

To discourage pilfering the firm might institute spot checks of the following:

- theoretical and actual stocks of specific items
- whether all the goods on outgoing trucks appear on materials issues documents
- individual storekeepers as they leave work. (Note that a firm which wishes to do this must incorporate a clause into the contract of employment between the worker and the firm giving the firm the right to stop and search workers as they leave the premises)
- whether all materials requisition slips have actually been signed by authorised persons
- whether materials issued to authorised persons have actually been used in work for the firm and not for personal use or benefit
- whether stores staff are taking their holiday entitlement. Workers who defraud their employers by improperly altering documents are usually reluctant to be away from work for fear that temporary replacements will uncover their theft.

Capacity planning

Capacity planning is the attempt to match the level of departmental activity to the level of demand for its output or services. You estimate the level of capacity needed to meet your output objectives and then control resources to ensure that this level of capacity exists. Thus, you establish job priorities and organise the flow of work so as to guarantee that top priority jobs are completed on time. CP could require, for example, that you forgo an increase in production to reserve resources for a major job that is waiting on the sidelines. Effective CP demands accurate forecasts of capacity use and availability, taking account of possible breakdowns. You have to know the demands likely to be placed on your department; yet the precision of this information depends largely on the predictive abilities of other sections. Always request this data in writing, and keep a copy of the memorandum. If someone asks you to deal with a major job urgently, have that person confirm the request in writing.

Short term capacity can sometimes be varied through

overtime working and the leasing of extra plant and equipment. Alternatively, a firm might deliberately maintain sufficient excess capacity to deal with any increase in demand that may reasonably be expected to arise. The choice will depend on the relative costs of overtime, leasing, sub-contracting, and the maintenance of spare capacity. Sometimes, workflows can be smoothed out by deferring or bringing forward the maintenance of equipment and by the rapid redeployment of labour between departments.

Other departmental planning duties could include 'layout planning', to determine the locations of plant and equipment which minimise the time spent moving work between processes and departments; and 'materials requirements planning' (MRP) whereby you schedule the provision of components and sub-assemblies in such a way that they all arrive on time for incorporation into the final item. MRP requires continuous monitoring of inventory levels to ensure that input requirements can be met, and that materials are issued in good time.

Controlling the plan

Plans need to be flexible and capable of continuous adjustment as circumstances change. Accordingly, control systems should be incorporated into plans in order to monitor their performance. If a plan begins to fail you need to know this quickly so that corrective action can be taken. Thus you require predetermined criteria for measuring 'success' and a feedback mechanism informing you when things go wrong. The best system of all is the 'closed loop' feedback mechanism whereby information on current performance automatically adjusts current operations in order to rectify divergences between planned and actual activity. Closed loop systems have had few managerial applications in the past because of administrative problems in collecting and analysing data. Today however they are increasingly feasible through use of standard programs on desktop computers. Thus, for example, the speed of a production line might automatically and instantly adjust itself according to the number of defectives it produces or inventories might be automatically replenished as stock usage rates increase. 'Open loop' systems in contrast are feedback mechanisms that do require human intervention. They are sufficiently flexible to accommodate changing circumstances, but remain constant unless someone takes the initiative to implement an alteration.

Feedback information may be supplied in the form of ratios, graphs or charts, or documents (inspection reports, delivery notes etc).

The management of change

There are of course those who avoid planning, preferring instead to react to events. This avoids the costs and inconveniences of planning, recognises the enormous difficulties of forecasting the future, but leaves the organisation vulnerable to the effects of change. The management of change requires an understanding of its causes, consequences and implications for current behaviour. The organisation may then attempt to eliminate problems before they occur, but in so doing risks eliminating activities that might actually help in the future rather than hinder.

To many people, the term 'managing change' means implementing redundancies and, regrettably, industrial change does often manifest itself in this way. 'Human resource planning' (HRP) can help avoid redundancy. HRP requires that the firm compares its existing labour resources with forecast labour demand and then schedules a series of activities for acquiring, training and perhaps redeploying workers. If your department employs staff on various standard company-wide grades, ask the personnel department for an estimate of labour turnover within each of the grades. Then assess the implications of high or low turnover rates on the work of your department. Ask the personnel officer to give you plenty of warning of possible changes in working hours, holiday entitlements, union agreements on working practices etc that could affect your schedules. You should then be able to predict the future recruitment, training and (possibly) redundancy requirements of your department and thus devise plans for handling the human problems that arise from labour deficits or surpluses.

Often, natural wastage and redeployment can remove the need for redundancies, but for effective redeployment to be possible you need to know exactly what each of your subordinates is able to do. Consider therefore the possibility of preparing a 'skills inventory' of all the attributes, qualifications and experiences possessed by each of your staff. This will require your asking people about aspects of their backgrounds not strictly relevant to their current jobs and staff may resent such questions. Yet, the information you gather can enable you to assess each person's suitability for alternative work. Discretion is required here, since the dividing line between occupationally relevant questions and unjustifiable prying into confidential personal affairs is often thin.

Change emanates from new technology, from organisational restructuring, and from alterations in working systems or methods. There are new products and materials, while the political, cultural, economic and legal frameworks within which firms operate are liable to rapid alteration. Organisations, as they mature, typically become more formal, bureaucratic and set in their ways. To the extent that firms themselves initiate change they can control and modify its consequences. Thus, some large businesses make one or more senior managers specifically responsible for the identification of problem areas requiring change, and for its implementation. These individuals monitor external events and assess their implications for existing administrative structures. They are particularly concerned to predict (and if possible avoid) redundancies. Adjustment to change will be easier the wider the skills, experiences and responsibilities of employees, implying of course that job extension and enrichment are appropriate policies for firms operating in fast changing technical and market environments.

You should encourage the acceptance of change. Recognise, however, that resistance to change is inevitable when jobs, status, privileges or incomes are threatened. Pay and other relativities can alter, personal relationships may be upset, skills acquired through great effort over many years might no longer be relevant. Good communications are crucial — you need to explain carefully to subordinates the need for various changes and their expected consequences. Where possible, avoid disrupting existing workgroups since loyalty to a group can be a powerful agent of change. Of course, interpersonal relationships must alter as one working environment replaces another, but efficient groups should not be broken up simply for change's sake.

Fears of redundancy or redeployment (accompanied by loss of status, a move to another geographical area, disruption of relationships etc) are perhaps the greatest impediment to the smooth introduction of new methods. And workers need to be reassured that the organisation has their best interests at heart. This might be achieved by the firm visibly creating a financial reserve specifically intended to protect employees from the adverse consequences of unforeseen change. These funds might be used to retrain employees in new skills, pay the moving expenses of workers who need to be redeployed, and perhaps compensate older employees who prefer to take early retirement rather than retrain in new technology.

Summary

Planning takes place at many different levels within an organisation and the larger the company, the more difficult it is to coordinate activities.

You have seen how corporate planning can give the central theme around which all other planning activities can revolve. However, at the end of the day, planning is about getting information that is accurate and reliable, and using your skill as a manager to interpret that information and devise plans. New technology does not remove the need for human involvement.

Cast a critical eye over the planning procedures of your own company. Identify ways in which they could be improved.

9
Negotiation

Objectives

This chapter will help you to:

- develop the skills associated with negotiation
- explain the importance of developing formal procedures
- identify the techniques used in conducting negotiations.

Negotiation is an important management skill and it is essential that you be able to negotiate effectively. You might negotiate with union officials, safety representatives, with colleagues in committees, with other departments and possibly with customers and suppliers. Negotiation enters into interpersonal relations with subordinates via performance appraisal and management by objectives interviews, the implementation of work study exercises and in grievance control. Negotiation differs from consultation in that, whereas consultation results in a unilateral decision imposed by yourself (albeit taking into account the views of your subordinates), negotiation implies decision taking through agreements which both sides are obliged to keep. Typically, consultation is not adequate for subjects that involve conflict and/or deeply divided views. The essence of negotiation is compromise; you seek the agreement of the other side to the maximum number of your demands. Willingness to negotiate presupposes a willingness to forego various objectives — there is little point offering to negotiate if you are totally inflexible in your aims. It is important therefore to distinguish clearly between issues on which you will negotiate and those about which you are prepared only to consult. When negotiating, you need to predetermine how far you are prepared to go in meeting the other side's requests and you must learn not to accumulate too many enemies at any one time.

Self-check

What is the difference between consultation and negotiation?

Answer
Negotiation implies a willingness to compromise and joint decision-making, whereas consultation requires the manager to discuss matters with subordinates, but leaves the final decision with the manager, who can impose it if necessary.

To bargain effectively you need a clearly defined set of negotiating objectives, a thorough understanding of the feelings and motives of the other side and a well prepared negotiating plan which sets out the strategy and tactics you intend to adopt. Your strategy will depend on the resources at your disposal and the implications and expected repercussions of various solutions to the issue — the outcome from one negotiation sets precedents for others. The other side might offer concessions that assuage some of the difficulties created by its demands. Your aim therefore is to balance the costs and benefits of different outcomes, ensuring that you are left no worse off by the eventual settlement. Professional approaches to negotiation involve detailed analysis not only of negotiating environments and situations, but also of the personal characteristics of the individuals representing the other side. Take this seriously, because in non-trivial negotiations (especially those which involve outside bodies) it is *extremely* likely that your opponents will be analysing you — amateurism is an expensive luxury here. Analyse the opposition's case, the justifications for its position, the costs of conceding to its demands and the extent of the opposition's support from other parties (eg support for union representatives on the part of the union rank and file). Check the validity of the facts the opposition is likely to put forward in support of its claim. What does the opposition *really* want and how far is it prepared to go in securing its objectives?

The dilemma facing negotiators is that if on the one hand they are totally Machiavellian, their opponents will disbelieve *everything* they say, whereas to trust the opposition invites double-cross and unsatisfactory outcomes. If you are blatantly suspicious of your opponents, challenging and/or denying every statement they make, then you will not create an environment conducive to constructive negotiation, especially if the other party is negotiating in good faith. You need, therefore, to assess the integrity of your opponents as well as their payoffs if you concede. Indeed, it may be that you like and respect your opponent — negotiators can be embarrassed by the conflicts of personal interest that negotiating situations sometimes provide. Supervisors, for instance, may greatly prefer the company of the shop stewards with whom they regularly negotiate over grievance and disciplinary matters, working practices, bonus rates etc than the company of other managers. Parties to a negotiation share common experiences, interact socially and develop 'ongoing' relationships. This may expedite negotiations but might not benefit the negotiators' principals: friendships between individuals could cause them not to extract the maximum possible concessions from the other side, particularly if bad personal relationships would result.

There is much ritual associated with negotiation: people who have known each other for many years may behave unusually when 'negotiating' and the protocols that individuals perceive as proper for a negotiation can, by inducing stuffy, overformal atmospheres, themselves impede agreement and excessive for-mality can cause individual negotiators to overestimate their own importance in the proceedings.

You represent management; yet you might not agree with the settlements your superiors expect you to achieve and they might continually increase their expectations of your ability to deliver advantageous outcomes. Never underestimate to your superiors the difficulty of an impending negotiation. Point out the problems and, where appropriate, the sanctions available to the other side. Offer conservative estimates of attainable outcomes and establish precisely how far you are allowed to go in independently altering your negotiating objectives as discussions proceed. While it is generally unwise to keep referring back to your principals as the negotiating climate alters, do ensure that you have immediate access (normally by telephone) to someone who is able to take policy decisions.

Activity

What negotiating procedures are used by your organisation? Try to imagine that you are describing them to an outsider.

The next part of the chapter will consider the different negotiating situations and suggest how to deal with them. Try to relate this to your own experience as far as possible.

Negotiating procedures

There are three types of negotiating situation: conjunctive, where parties have no alternative but to settle, distributive, involving the sharing out of a fixed amount of resources or rewards and 'integrative', whereby the parties seek jointly agreed positions. Negotiating machinery must be tailored to suit particular circumstances; there are no set rules. It would be silly to use the same mechanisms for allocating the departmental budget as for settling a major industrial dispute. However, certain general guidelines apply to the efficient administration of all negotiations:

- the size of the bargaining unit should depend on its ability to implement agreed decisions. For instance, there is little point in a workplace union representative negotiating a pay increase for his or her members with (say) a departmental supervisor who is not empowered to deliver the agreed award. A 'bargaining unit' is the domain to which a collective agreement applies, eg a department or division of a firm, a subsidiary of a company, etc

- matters for which a bargaining unit will be responsible should be predetermined. Decisions on subjects to be included in negotiations might themselves require preliminary negotiation
- all parties with a vested interest in the outcome of a negotiation should be represented on the negotiating team
- a timetable for completing the negotiation should be established in advance (to encourage progress towards a settlement)
- rules governing the order of debate, methods of presentation, when questions shall be asked etc should (where possible) be determined in advance.

Moreover, certain conventions have emerged which facilitate efficient bargaining. These are that once an offer has been made it should remain on the table until the situation changes or unless it was made conditional on some reciprocity that is not forthcoming; that all aspects of items on the agenda shall be negotiable, unless one of the parties has previously indicated its unwillingness to discuss certain matters; that negotiators should negotiate only with each other and not make secret appeals to the people the other side represents; and that confidential conversations between opposing representatives shall not be repeated during formal negotiations. Observance of these simple rules puts neither side at any disadvantage, yet creates a robust and professional working environment.

Negotiations are most efficient when conducted dispassionately. There should be no personal abuse, each party's case should be stated clearly and politely with points of agreement and dispute plainly identified. Usually, proceedings begin with one of the parties (normally the side which initiated the negotiation) making an opening statement outlining its objectives and offering facts and opinions designed to convince the opponent of the justice of its case. If you are the person who opens the discussions, then begin by stating your perceptions of the issue and suggest a solution. Do not specify how much you are willing to concede or impose any final demands. Experienced negotiators recognise that negotiations rarely involve 'all or nothing' situations and even if your case is strong you should always allow your opponent to 'save face'.

Self-check

While rigid rules are to be avoided, there are four conventions that should be followed. What are they?

Answer
— an offer should remain on the table unless circumstances change or it was conditional and the condition has not been met
— all items on the agenda are negotiable unless one party has declared otherwise
— none of the parties should attempt to make secret deals
— any confidential discussions between opposing parties should not be repeated during formal discussions.

The main purpose of these conventions is to create a professional working environment.

Before the meeting, assess your opponent's attitudes towards the issue, the strengths and weaknesses of its case, the abilities of its representatives and their background knowledge of you and the issue. Estimate the extent of their opposition to your proposals and prepare a list of the arguments they are likely to put forward, including objections to your own position. Deliver the opening statement enthusiastically and with conviction. Deal with the more obvious objections to your statements during the introduction, state the facts as you see them, quoting examples and precedents and emphasise the strongest aspects of your case. Predict in advance questions likely to arise from your opening statement and provide answers to them before they are asked. The other side then makes its presentation and bargaining ensues.

You have to distinguish between 'primary' and 'secondary' demands. The former are demands over which no concessions are possible, the latter are subject to compromise. No negotiator can realistically expect to achieve all his or her demands, so priorities must be established and some objectives relegated to a subsidiary role. Choice of primary demands is necessarily subjective (the inclusion of some may require abandonment of others) and note how the friendship or enmity of other participants in 'multilateral' negotiations depends crucially on the choice of primary demands — the relegation of a primary demand to secondary status can turn enemies into friends and vice versa. Pacts and liaisons between one pair of participants in a negotiation can create suspicion and hostility among the rest. Clearly, it might be wise to play down some interests simply to dampen opposition — demands must be chosen tactfully and the enthusiasm with which they are pursued varied as circumstances change.

The side making the initial opening statement has an advantage in that it can determine the general context in which the negotiations take place (their tone, the way in which subjects are discussed, coverage of issues and so on). It is important that you do not respond to your opponent's opening statement hurriedly or in a manner that relates more to his or her presentation than to your own predetermined position. If it is clear that the two sides see the situation from entirely different perspectives you should *still* proceed with your prepared opening statement. Not only will this emphasise the differences in your positions, but it also gives you time to absorb the introductory comments of the other side. Do not make a counter offer at this stage — to do so legitimizes your opponent's aspirations. Make your offer at the end, not the beginning, of a negotiation and always set your initial offer within the limits of your predetermined strategy.

A common, though reprehensible, tactic is to agree to a demand in general terms but deliberately fail to establish procedures whereby the settlement can be implemented. Several months then elapse before the non-implementation is noticed and more time passes before complaints are registered. By then, the personnel involved in the original agreement might have left the organisation and new negotiations to secure its implementation have to begin all over again. At these new discussions, the party that initially agreed to the demand might argue that circumstances have changed and that the terms of the settlement can no longer apply.

Self-check

What is the significance of primary and secondary demands?

Answer
Primary demands are those where no concessions are possible while secondary demands are open to discussion.

Since no side can expect to achieve all the demands made, it is essential for all those representing the side to agree on those issues where a compromise might be possible and those where no concessions can be made.

Never make offers without fully understanding their implications. Demands and offers should be stated specifically, preferably in quantifiable terms. Each demand must be supported by a substantive argument, containing a succession of logically presented points. Silence is a useful weapon in debate: argument causes adrenalin to flow in both parties — a brief silence can defuse the potency of the other side's previous remark. If you cannot answer a point put to you, restate it in a slightly different way, adding a new dimension to which you can in fact respond. This enables you to wear down the other side until the original vexing point is either forgotten or distorted. Of course, the other side may raise points which, logically, cause you to change your mind. You need time to consider, so do not make hasty concessions. Say you will return to the point later in the discussion, but then introduce enough additional material into the argument to justify a break following its (lengthy) presentation. Reconsider your basic position during the break.

A common variation on this theme is the practice (common in pay negotiations with unions) of management agreeing to discuss a certain issue, but insisting that other items appear on the agenda of the meeting at which the issue is discussed. Consider for example a firm that announces redundancies without first consulting the recognised union. The union demands a meeting with the management to voice opposition to the proposals. Management agrees, but suggests that some related topics be dealt with at the same time. The redundancy question is placed towards the end of the agenda following other innocuous looking items. When discussing these early items management introduces matters relating to the financial difficulties of the firm and the need for improved efficiency. It then asks, innocently, for comment and for suggestions on how the situation might be alleviated. Union negotiators, unwittingly, then begin to discuss the proposed redundancies in the context of a broader situation the parameters of which have been defined by the other side. Management leads the discussion towards the conclusion that jobs are actually being saved by making a few people redundant. The fact that management behaved improperly (and illegally) in failing to consult prior to announcing redundancies and in not following the statutory procedure is forgotten as the parallel issues are considered. Another difficulty with multi-topic agendas is that an agreement on one item might become conditional on the achievement of a settlement on another and to secure the latter you might have to make unanticipated undesirable concessions. Agenda items are 'traded off' against each other.

Deflecting the opposition from its original purpose is one of many 'professional fouls' employed by skilled and determined negotiators. Some other commonly used 'tricks of the trade' are listed below:

- conceding the existence of weaknesses in a certain proposition and then offering compromises based on *your* interpretation of their significance
- creating diversions and systematically confusing seemingly clear issues
- criticising the motives of the person presenting the argument rather than discussing the issue or giving reasons for decisions
- insisting that a certain practice is common in other firms, industries or situations when in fact it is not
- congratulating the other side on the logic of its arguments, flattering the incisive rationality of its presentation but then suggesting conclusions to these arguments which directly contradict the opponent's position
- introducing irrelevancies into the argument, drawing false

analogies, and putting words into the other party's mouth knowing full well he or she will object and then waste time in correcting your (knowingly) false interpretations of their statements

- deliberately confusing an issue to such an extent that it seems reasonable to establish a subcommittee to investigate and deal with its implications. The establishment of a subcommittee is usually fatal for the problem under discussion
- presenting one's own unashamedly disgraceful behaviour as the consequence of a carefully considered, rationally justified moral position
- making broad generalisations knowing they will be challenged. Selecting untypical particular instances to 'prove a point'.

Clearly, lasting and satisfactory agreements are possible only if the parties negotiate in good faith. There are innumerable ways to disrupt and undermine negotiations and disruptive tactics may themselves be a part of the negotiating strategy of one (or both) of the sides. Be aware of these unpleasant (but common) manoeuvres, but recognise that they are ultimately destructive — they may result in short term 'victory' for one of the participants, yet might fail in the longer term as other parties realise they were duped and hence retaliate. You should adopt a *principled* approach. Do not provoke your opponents. Treat them with courtesy and respect, yet be fully aware of the tricks they might pull.

Keep cool, control your temper and never initiate a personal attack. Stick to the subject of the negotiations and do not respond to personal criticism or abuse. Remain silent if someone shouts or swears at you, look directly at the assailant, count to five then lift your pen horizontally about a foot above your notes, stare at the pen for two seconds maintaining your silence, then drop it onto the desk and say, slowly:

I think the usefulness of this discussion has come to an end. I came here in good faith to conduct a negotiation, I did not come here to be abused and insulted. Good day.

Activity

How do you react if someone is abusive towards you or subjects you to personal criticism?

Tempting as it may be to retaliate in some way, you should avoid this course of action as it achieves little.

If it happens to you, try the approach outlined in the next section.

Then leave, even if the person insulting you apologises. If there is any point in continuing the discussion you can always fix a time for reconvening the meeting at a later date and you can insist that the person who abused you apologise in writing before the new meeting. You gain nothing by trying to continue negotiating in an angry frame of mind.

Be patient and seek positively to accommodate the other side. Give clear reasons for rejecting outright any of its proposals. Remember always that the other side might have available to it some powerful sanction that it has not revealed and if you stubbornly refuse a request now only to accede totally when the sanction is threatened you destroy your credibility for future negotiations. Do not admit mistakes too freely. If you are obviously in the wrong then promise to investigate the matter later and if your position is in fact hopeless use the politician's well known device of simply saying that 'important lessons have been learned'. During protracted negotiations, pause occasionally to check your understanding of the other side's position and where necessary to clarify and expand your own. Summarise your interpretation of the present state of the discussion and ask the other side if it agrees. Do not interrupt your opponent's presentation, but do make notes of the weakest aspects of his or her case.

Once an agreement has been reached, insist that it be written down and that named persons be made responsible for its implementation. Set a timetable for the activities needed to execute the agreement and establish a procedure for monitoring progress towards the goal. Settlements should of course be implemented in the form in which they were agreed.

Self-check

Having reached an agreement, why should it be written down and a timetable for implementation drawn up?

Answer

It is always advisable for all parties to agree the wording of an agreement, in order to avoid problems later on. Similarly, the drawing up of an action plan to implement the agreement will increase the likelihood of success. It will enable all parties to monitor events.

The skills you need

Supervisory managers will be most concerned with negotiations relating to grievance and disciplinary systems and with the *interpretation* of agreements on terms and conditions of employment. The latter will normally be subject to management/union collective bargaining, in which more senior managers are involved. Nevertheless, the skills needed for collective bargaining are fundamentally similar to those used for negotiating agreements to minor disputes. The technique of 'behaviour analysis' involves your seeking to isolate, analyse and measure the behaviour of the other side. Thus you (or a colleague who accompanies you) should record the incidence of the following categories of behaviour in your opponent:

- making a proposal
- developing a proposal made by someone else
- registering disagreement
- defending or attacking others
- stating difficulties or otherwise blocking proposals
- admitting mistakes and/or inadequacies
- testing other people's understanding
- summarising previous discussions
- asking questions
- offering information
- interrupting others
- consciously involving other people in a discussion.

In consequence, you build up a databank on your opponents' behaviour. There are, of course, practical problems with behaviour analysis:

- it is sometimes difficult to categorise a behaviour accurately, particularly when several specified behaviours occur simultaneously (eg a question which interrupts someone else, blocks a proposal and registers disagreement)
- even when you have collected this data it might not help you in the negotiation, since the power of one of the parties is often the overriding consideration in determining outcomes
- numerous extra categories of behaviour relevant to negotiation may be defined — so many that it would not be physically possible to monitor all of them at the same time.

Nevertheless, conscious examination of opponents' behaviour during negotiations definitely enhances your awareness of the interpersonal relations that emerge during discussions, develops your capacity to respond quickly to altered negotiating circumstances and increases your sensitivity to the wider social environments in which negotiations occur. And it is not true that outcomes to negotiations depend only on the relative power of each of the participants independent of social interactions. Were power to define all outcomes then powerful parties would always win, which is obviously not actually the case.

Practise your negotiating skills. Choose at first easy situations where the consequences of failure are small. Take some interdepartmental conflict and seek to negotiate a solution. Then select another dispute to resolve, concentrate on correcting your previously identified negotiating weaknesses and deliberately introduce two or three new negotiating techniques. As you try your hand at more and more negotiations you can gradually extend your repertoire of negotiating methods — add a couple each time you enter a discussion, always recording carefully and diligently the extent of their success.

Bluff, counter-bluff, hard words, threats of sanctions, loss of temper and occasional ingratiation are all part of the negotiation game. Expect them as a matter of course, but never lose sight of your fundamental objectives. Such devices are acceptable (indeed inevitable) provided you consciously separate the problems under discussion from the personalities of the people presenting opposing views and provided you focus on solutions rather than participants.

Activity

What skills and attributes will a good negotiator display?

The basic skill of a good negotiator is meticulous planning and preparation both prior and during the negotiations. Careful preparation of the case to be put and responses to possible questions and problems put forward by the other side mean that you will convey an image of being self-confident.

You may have included other factors such as persuasive, assertive, ability to convey ideas, good public speaking etc. These and others are outlined in the next part of the chapter.

Negotiating techniques

Good negotiators plan their tactics meticulously. They recognise the importance of communications, of body language, persuasive advocacy and all other aspects of effective presentation and they are always in control of their own behaviour. As a negotiator, you need to collect and analyse all the facts available on the disputed issue, to list your objectives and study the objectives of the other side. Highlight points of agreement and differences between the two positions and how disagreements might be resolved. Write out the feasible solutions that you would *least* and *most* like to see imposed. Try empathising with the other side. Why do they feel as they do? What is the root cause of the conflict? Can disparate opinions be united to further the pursuit of a common, mutually beneficial goal?

A common problem in management/worker negotiations is the inability of one side to understand how the other feels it ought to behave. For example, it has been argued that in industrial relations bargaining, managements and unions *perceive* situations in entirely different ways.[1] Management might assume there are no inherent conflicts of interest in industry, while unions simultaneously assume that fundamental conflicts do in fact exist. Thus, management regards collective effort towards achievement of common goals by a united, disciplined workforce as the natural state of affairs. Those in command are not able, therefore, to comprehend the motives behind challenges to managerial authority. If people are considered as members of a team striving jointly to achieve greater rewards for all, with existing managers as team leaders, then 'disruptive' behaviour simply does not make sense. Cooperation is taken for granted; all dissent is viewed as unreasonable. It cannot even be understood! If however the firm's profits are regarded as something to be fought over, each side legitimately seeking to maximise its own reward, then industrial action to secure the largest possible share of revenues for the workforce is easily explained.

If colleagues are to assist you in a negotiation, brief them on the facts of the case and allocate a distinct role to each member of the team. Have them conduct research into earlier or similar cases and their outcomes. Look for precedents and customs relevant to the case. Good preparation is essential. Predict the impact on the other side of various methods of approach and define your fall-back position in respect of each disputed item.

In choosing a strategy, consider the capacities, intentions, motives and resources of the other side. What is its real (as opposed to stated) objectives? What sort of situation does it want to exist after a settlement is reached? Who will help the other party achieve its objectives; who will hinder and why? Does your opponent have 'allies'? If so, what do you need do to turn these allies against your opponent?

The 'climate' of a negotiation can suddenly change, particularly when either party alters its minimum conditions for a settlement or when conflicts or dissentions within a negotiating team emerge. A seemingly innocuous redefinition of primary demands or relegation of some demands to secondary status can create friends from enemies and alter instantly the environment in which discussions occur. Settlements rarely correspond to participants' prior expectations. Outcomes are uncertain: a short term gain can become a long term loss, as for example when a union wins an immediate pay rise which increases a firm's labour costs so much that redundancies become inevitable in the longer term. Equally a 'victory' of management in an industrial dispute might create bitterness and hostility which eventually negates the initial gain. Unforeseen pitfalls abound in the implementation of settlements. No result can be guaranteed.

Having defined fall-back positions beyond which they are not prepared to retreat, negotiators usually make bids in excess of what they are prepared to accept. Then haggling over specific issues occurs. If settlements do not emerge, the particular items preventing agreement might be isolated and set aside while other matters are discussed. Precise definition of a stumbling block can generate fresh insights into its substance and stimulate new ideas on how it might be overcome.

To bargain effectively, you must know how and when to barter. Advantages and concessions are tradeable commodities — indeed phoney concessions might be offered in order to relax opposition at crucial moments. The pace of a negotiation can be deliberately slowed down whenever the other side is winning a point and/or vital information can be withheld until the last possible instant. An opposition can be gradually disheartened and exhausted through intentionally breaking off negotiations when agreement seems near. Adjournments have beneficial and detrimental aspects: they give the opposition time to reassess its tactics, but also build up tension and anxiety during the interval.

You do not have to respond to every point the other party makes (some will be red herrings anyway) and make your opponent work hard for any point you concede. It is unwise to let the opposition know which of your demands are primary and which secondary, until you have heard their views, since you may on reflection feel that some of your secondary demands can now be safely promoted to primary status and vice versa.

State your arguments politely, directly and in simple terms. Where possible, relate your own proposals to those of your opponent, so that you can get the other side to have your

---

Self-check

What is meant by a fall back position and how might a barter system be used?

Answer

A fall back position is usually the minimum that a side is willing to accept. It is rather like selling a car. You advertise the car in the local paper asking for '£3,500 ono', knowing that you are willing to accept £3,000. The buyer may offer £2,500, though in fact is prepared to go as high as £3,200. At the end of the day, both parties have to feel that they have made a good deal.

In negotiations, you will often operate a barter system, whereby you concede one point if the other side will give way on another. Again, it is a face-saving exercise, a ritual associated with negotiations.

(rather than its) own way! Thank your opponents for their concessions and point out their usefulness in securing a solution (this might even encourage the opponents to put further concessions on the table). Typically, the opposition will be negotiating on behalf of other people as well as themselves and need to be able to 'sell' a settlement to their principals. If they cannot claim to have extracted something from *you* they may lose the confidence of those they represent and this might cause them to adopt a hard line during negotiations.

While you ought not to offer concessions too soon, you must at some point indicate (perhaps circumspectly) the range of solutions you are willing to consider. Look carefully at your opponent when doing this and try to spot any clues about which of the alternatives he or she would most like to accept. If in so doing you can identify the opponent's most favoured solution, do not put this 'on the table' until the end of the negotiations by which time you should have been able to extract some concessions from the other side. If you cannot interpret the other side's demands — ask! A direct question will undoubtedly lead to a direct answer, though the answer given may not be true. Moreover, press for clarification of contentious issues so that your opponent has to restate the position. In doing this the other side might shift the emphasis of its demands to include points to which you can offer a stronger response. Question also the assumptions on which the other party has based its case. Assumptions lead to conclusions and to challenge one is to challenge the other. Introduce to the discussion any relevant facts the other side has failed to mention and ask for comment.

All negotiations eventually end, if only with a failure to agree. Thus, both sides have an interest in establishing common ground. Look for analogies, precedents and how others have resolved similar issues. A useful way of approaching an agreement is to ask the other side the question, 'What would happen if . . .', and then proceed to outline certain concessions you *might* be prepared to offer (entirely without commitment at this stage) in return for various reciprocities. The opponent might then make a similar hypothetical proposal and you will both have a broad understanding of how a settlement might be achieved. Then you begin to trade concessions, hoping that the (minor) concessions you offer will be matched by more significant concessions from the other side. Your aim is to elicit major benefits at minor cost.

Remember always that the opponent expects to go away with *something* and that settlement is most unlikely without at least a minimal quid pro quo. Make your opponent's decisions easy: suggest alternative ways for presenting the settlement to the outside world, offer some interpretations of your proposals which make them appear beneficial to the opponent. Try to appear as having yielded to your opponent's pressure, even when you have not.

Summary

Having completed this chapter, you may feel that negotiations resemble a game, where each side is trying to outguess and outmanoeuvre the other.

Any newcomer has to learn the rules of the game in order to be successful and experience is the best teacher.

You will be expected to participate in negotiations, usually as a representative of management and part of a team. You must practise the techniques of planning, bargaining, analysis of behaviour etc.

In order to become a good negotiator, you must understand your own strengths and weaknesses and devise ways of acquiring/improving the skills you need.

Note

1 Fox, A, *Industrial Sociology and Industrial Relations*, Royal Commission on Trade Unions and Employers' Association Research Paper no 3, HMSO, 1966.

Index

Other titles in the Effective Supervisory Management Series

Managing People

Preface

1 **Recruitment, Selection and Induction**
Objectives — Recruitment — Selection methods — The problems involved — Employment interviewing — Induction — The exit (termination) interview

2 **Training**
Objectives — Evaluation — Training methods — Techniques of training — Computer based training — Group training — National Vocational Qualifications (NVQs) — Management training

3 **Performance Appraisal**
Objectives — Performance reviews — Critical incidents — Potential reviews — Reward reviews — Appraisal interviews — Usefulness of transactional analysis — Equal opportunities considerations — Further problems with performance appraisal — Legal aspects — The EOC Code of Practice

4 **Counselling**
Objectives — What counselling is — Counselling methods — Directive versus non-directive counselling — The counselling interview — Is counselling really worthwhile?

5 **Job Evaluation**
Objectives — Why have job evaluation? — Devising a scheme — Problems with job evaluation — Legal considerations — Measuring equal value through analytical job evaluation — Jobs that are not equal

6 **Handling Grievances**
Objectives — The need for formal procedures — The case for informality — A model grievance procedure — Causes of grievances — Dealing with grievances

Managing Activities and Resources

Preface